Don't Take My
Lemonade Stand
An American Philosophy

To the family & friends
of Dan & Diane.
Great Americans All!

We must take a
Stand for the Stand!
USA!

James Johnson
1/25/13
@jjauthor

Don't Take My Lemonade Stand

An American Philosophy

A Prescription for our Corrupt, Rigged, Flawed, and Squeezed Political System

Janie Johnson

An American Citizen

BASCOM HILL
PUBLISHING GROUP

Bascom Hill Publishing Group
212 3ʳᵈ Avenue North, Suite 290
Minneapolis, MN 55401
612.455.2293
www.bascomhillpublishing.com

Author website: www.jjauthor.com
Author email: jjauthor@gmail.com

ISBN 10: 978-1-935098-29-4
ISBN 13: 1-935098-29-2
LCCN: 2010904741

Jacket photography: Jurgen Reisch
Book Design: Ghislain Viau
Illustrations: Roy Wilson
Book Jacket: Chris Collins
Website by Monte Hershberger/Etnom.com

Printed in the United States of America

To my mother and to all of our children

Table of Contents

Part III: The Origins and Foundations of Liberalism/Progressivism

Part IV: The Practical Applications of Conservative Principles to Current Issues

Part V: A Call to Action 285

Acknowledgment

Thanks to Debbie Lanni for her encouragement and help with the title. I want to send a special thanks to my friends Kris Erb and Terry LaLonde. Kris had the nerve to review and edit my very first rough draft. Terry is a neighbor and a bountiful source of Conservative wisdom. Scott Bennion provided a consistent touch of satire, irreverence, and intellectual honesty. Terry Ballas supported me with his usual creativity and marketing sense. Sharon Hermann and Wendy Froggett, editor and graphic artist respectively, were there for me at times when the task of writing seemed overwhelming. Joe McDermott, an old friend, always gave me his honest appraisal from his artist's perspective. Roy Wilson created all of my wonderful and professional illustrations.

My family and my friends have been supportive throughout. My husband and his brother, Uncle Steve (and his wife, Karen), provided constant critiquing and daily support. My brothers Brent and Timmy and my sister Maylin helped with all their suggestions, encouragement, and prayers when their little sister told them she was going to write a book. Thank you to my amazing Aunt Mary and Uncle Chris (Boston) for all their love and support not just for this book, but for my entire life. Kathy Jackson, Chris Forvilly, PJ Sapp, Karen Shin, Wendy Caragher, Maria McNamara, and Mary Swisher have been the best of friends throughout the writing process.

And most of all, I want to send the most special thanks of all to our children, Steve, Joe, Tom, Matthew, Patrick, Michael, and Sammy (the lucky one).

Note from the Author

Where We Are

Government policies are arguably wrong, but the political process is surely corrupt.

Policy

Big government is squeezing:

- the Constitution
- U.S. currency
- American individual liberties
- U.S. Defense efforts
- the judicial system
- Free-Market Capitalism
- free speech
- morality
- the need for self-reliance and personal responsibility
- funding for entrepreneurs
- private-sector opportunities
- fiscal responsibility

How are they doing it?

- unnecessary regulations
- taxes so high as to create barriers and reduce incentives
- Federal Reserve bailouts and money printing

- judicial activists who ignore the law and the Constitution in favor of their own version of social justice
- government redistribution of wealth
- attacks on successful businesses
- expanded government bureaucracies
- attacks on property rights
- abuse of environmental laws
- failures of government institutions (e.g., schools, DMV, Postal Service, IRS, etc.)
- rampant political deception
- weak foreign policy
- and more

Process

The political class is filled with self-serving politicians on both sides of the aisle. The political system is corrupt and rigged against everyday citizens in favor of special interests, reelection for politicians, big campaign contributors, and political friends and family. Everyday citizens are regularly betrayed by

- backroom deals
- "legal" bribes for senators to buy votes
- bills that go on for more than a thousand pages and overlong tax codes designed specifically to hide advantages given to favored constituencies
- lobbyists
- omnibus bills built for deception
- hidden earmarks for senior legislators
- falsely named legislation
- vague and unspecific legislative language designed as a gift to trial attorneys
- purposeful deceit at nearly all levels of government

We the People

We the people have the obligation as American citizens to take control of both government policies and the political process. Everyone might not be in agreement on all policy issues, but we all agree that political corruption and deception is wrong and needs our immediate attention. Everyone wants to fund a safety net for those truly infirm or in need, but no one wants to be on the wrong side of a rigged process. No one wants to carry the burden for freeloaders who should carry their own load. No one wants to pay for hidden favors to big campaign contributors or special interests. No one wants to vote for a candidate who says one thing on the campaign trail but does another when in office. As American citizens, we cannot continue to say, "That's just the way it's done" or "Everyone does it." All just power of our government is derived from the people, and now is the time for we the people to take back some of that power.

Where We Need to Be

Peace and prosperity are not inconsistent with Common Sense Conservative principles, integrity, and transparency. We as American citizens must make it so.

—Janie Johnson, An American Citizen

Preface

We the People . . . If we the people do not engage in the politics of life and government, who will? If we the people do not instruct our children how to take over for us when it is their turn, who will? If we the people do not get involved in government policy and take the initiative to put integrity and honor back into the political process, who will? Sadly, we know the answers to these questions. If it is anyone, it will be the zealots who can do little else that we will send to Washington to represent us. It will be those who are glib and can turn a compelling phrase, regardless of their inexperience or lack of skills or radical philosophies, who will be elected. It will be those who give speeches offering integrity and transparency on the campaign trail but willingly participate in the corrupt political process soon after they take office. And who, if not us, will prepare our children for the future that will soon be theirs? We know the answer: it will be someone who does not share our values, someone who has not learned from history, some imperious politician who takes his or her cues from our corrupt political process. Unless we the people actively engage in the process of governing our country and teaching our children our values and principles of life, the experience and lessons of our founding fathers on both

If We Don't Teach Them, They Won't Learn, and If They Don't Learn, They Will Not Be Ready to Finish What We Have Started!

Each new generation born is in effect an invasion of civilization by little barbarians, who must be civilized before it is too late.
—*Thomas Sowell*

government policy and political process could be lost forever. Our political system will stay rigged against everyday American citizens in favor of those in power and those close to them.

The whole process of writing this book began with one question from my very own ten-year-old barbarian. He asked, "How do you know who to vote for?"

I answered simply, "Whoever is for more individual liberty, whoever makes government smaller, and whatever does not give more money and power to the government, which is usually a Republican or someone with Conservative values."

Then Sammy asked, "Are you a Republican or a Democrat?"

I told him, "I am a registered Republican, but my political philosophy is Conservative. People often confuse Conservatives with Republicans, but not all Republicans are conservative, and not all Conservatives are Republicans." Looking into his big, brown eyes, I could see he was trying to understand what I was saying. "Sammy," I said, "the concept of being Conservative can get confusing. In the past, it generally meant that if one was a Republican, he or she was also a Conservative and vice versa but not anymore. Conservatism is a political philosophy or a way of thinking about government and life, and being a Republican reflects having a political party affiliation." I soon realized that everyday citizens, including me, Sammy, and millions of our nation's children needed to learn more about our country's history; the Conservative principles of our founding fathers; and where, when, and why Conservatism started.

Most of us are just everyday citizens taking care of our families and working on day-to-day issues. Count me in this group. We are not political scientists, historians, pundits, academics, special-interest groups, constitutional lawyers, or politicians, nor do we need to be. The history of our country is available to all of us in detail or in summary. We are all born with a conscience and the capacity to reason. All we need is the motivation and commitment to focus on historical results, current-day needs, and the needs of our children and our country. Although it is time consuming, it is not difficult for everyday people to develop a sound life and political philosophy based on what is right and what is wrong, on what has worked and what has not. With hard work, thorough research, common sense, compassion, reason, and morality, we can all know as much as the "experts" and develop our own philosophy of life and politics.

The pundits and other experts have written quite a lot commenting on life, politics, and government, and there is an important place for these books and articles. I recommend that you read and learn from them (see appendix). Their perspectives are important and meaningful, and in many ways, their views coincide with mine or have created a platform for me to build upon. However, although the philosophy and principles reflected in this book were developed on the shoulders of our founders and other modern-day thinkers, the final perspective here is that of just one mom who has taken the time to research our country's founding, the principles upon which our nation was built, and our children's and country's needs.

I do not purport to speak for all citizens or even all parents. I derived and developed the comments and notions expressed in this book over a long time from many sources. The purpose of having principles and theories is to help organize thought, and the ultimate purpose of organized thought is to help in deciding a course of action. The best way to answer Sammy's question, "How do you know who to vote for?" is to set a good example for our children by doing our homework, developing our own set of principles, and using these principles to make everyday decisions while we engage in the process of how our children are being educated and how our country is being governed. We need to take a stand for Common Sense Conservative policies and against the current rigged political process. Plus, we need to help our children develop the right set of principles and theories so they can determine the right course of action on their own. These lessons will not be about Republicans or Democrats because either can be Liberal or Conservative, and either can execute the duties of his or her office with integrity or dishonor. This education will be about children, country, and life. It will focus on Conservative versus Liberal philosophies of life and politics, and integrity versus corruption in the political process. My hope is that all citizens (especially other parents and my own children) will organize their thoughts and develop their own set of principles to allow them to think for themselves and develop their own life and political philosophies. It will be then that they can and will determine their own call to action!

I decided it was time for me to organize my own thoughts right here and right now to help educate and encourage everyday people to accept their responsibilities and obligations as American citizens to keep our politics honest and our country free and prosperous. I needed to make this call to action clear for Sammy and my other boys, as well as for all other parents to pass along to their children. That is how and why the real work on *Don't Take My Lemonade Stand, An American Philosophy* began.

Introduction

We *the people* have the capacity to return our country to the land of opportunity where we can expect our children to live in peace and prosperity. *We the people* are the captains of our own ships and the masters of our own destinies. *We the people* have the power. *We the people* have the opportunity and the obligation to use that power to improve circumstances for our children, our fellow citizens, and ourselves. It is the strength and power of *we the people* that will allow us to take back our country through reason, lessons learned from history, diligence, and the philosophy of Common Sense Conservatism.

Common Sense Conservatism is similar to other forms of Conservatism in that they both focus on morality, support for Capitalism, expanded individual liberties, and limited government. They differ in that Common Sense Conservatism puts a spotlight on three principle issues: children, patriotism, and optimism. Common Sense Conservatism begins by looking at all issues through the prism of what is best for our children. It addresses actions for today, but its focus is on the results that will be achieved tomorrow. The second tenet of Common Sense Conservatism, patriotism, goes beyond the notion of support of country and a willingness to defend it. It also includes a very favorable view of our country. Unlike the many who blame our country for most of the ills in the world, Common Sense Conservatism sees our country not as perfect, but as a noble liberator and provider of opportunity that is striving to do the right thing. The third tenet of Common Sense Conservatism, optimism, sees a positive future for our country and our children. It understands that from time to time our country leaves the path laid by its founders, but it believes in the goodness and ingenuity of our people and the potential for our children (with a little help from their parents) to place us back on the right track.

The primary message of this book is a call to action for everyday citizens to recognize the state of our country and the corruption

Join the Fight: Engage in the Process Right Here and Right Now to Save America

Teach Your Kids the History, Principles, and Practical Applications of Common Sense Conservatism

in our political process, to educate themselves in the lessons of history, to engage in how our country is being governed, and to make a difference. We the people have the power to do this if only we have the will.

In support of the book's secondary mission, to prepare our children for the future, this book goes beyond the narrow questions of political philosophy and includes simplified "Lemonade Stand" sections containing questions, examples, parables, illustrations, and kids' questions to better enable parents to educate their kids to think for themselves. Although the lemonade stand is a metaphor for individual liberties and rights, the true focus of the book is not on politics; it is on life. This book is the story of how we can not only engage in the governing process right here and now, but also how we can and need to use discussions of history, values, and character to inform and guide ourselves and our children. The future peace and prosperity of America is in our hands. However, in the not-too-distant future, our country's peace and prosperity will be in the hands of our children, and it is our responsibility to prepare them for this task.

In this book, I attempt to provide a basic, common sense understanding of Conservatism to anyone of any age and any education level. I will explain why this way of thinking is simply the best way to run our government and to enjoy life. This book reflects uniquely American principles and the common sense philosophy I use to make my everyday decisions that I want others, including my children, to know and understand. My hope is that reading this book will rouse interest, create curiosity, and motivate constructive action.

Philosophy is common sense with big words.

—James Madison

After my initial discussion with my ten-year-old, Sammy, about voting decisions, the next time we all sat down at the dinner table, I took the opportunity to begin what would become regular dialogues for our family about our own Common Sense Conservative principles, and why some fight so hard against them. I began these dialogues with this question:

What is it that Conservatism attempts to conserve? *Conservatism attempts to conserve and protect the individual rights, federal government limitations, and the moral values and principles presented by our founders in the Declaration of Independence and formally documented in the U.S. Constitution.*

As you might expect, my kids understood all of these words, but they did not find this definition all that meaningful. I found that explaining Conservatism in academic terms was not effective in part because it often seemed to make the points feel like homework. The primary mission of this book is to inform all Americans about the state of our country and the corruption embedded in our political process. I want to encourage everyday citizens to educate themselves and engage in how we are governed, to get them interested in the political process, and to teach the principles they have developed to their kids. The secondary mission of this book is to facilitate parental teaching. If the process of how our country is being governed were to be called a "game" (perhaps the most important game in the world), then the mission of this book might be stated as follows: *Inform and educate yourself. Get in the game, and teach your children so they will be ready when it is time for them to play.* It was during my review of the dual mission of the book that I decided that my message to parents could be expressed using straightforward, everyday language that focused on history, philosophy, and common sense, but that the same message might better relate to kids if it were presented in pithy or humorous illustrations and stories in conjunction with the adult text.

Conservatism was not made out of thin air.

It is rooted in freedom, and individual freedom
never goes out of style.

To help Sammy and all children better understand the historic
and current-day significance of Common Sense Conservative principles and values, several parables are presented throughout the
book. I call them parables not because they have anything directly
to do with religion, but because each parable presents a moral lesson
while it offers a bit of history and philosophy. The text provides

the logic and the history behind the principles, the illustrations present talking points for kids, and the parables marry the two by providing brief stories with moral lessons. All three of these forms of presentation are intended to inform, facilitate education, and offer compelling reasons for engagement.

The Fight Continues . . .

Today it is important for citizens throughout our country to recognize that the story and the fight relating to Conservative versus Progressive values and the fight relating to honest versus deceptive political processes continues. Liberals and Conservatives (and honor versus corruption) come with both Republican and Democrat brands. Sammy's story, and the story for all the children of our nation, will have a happy ending only when our country's citizens demand transparency and forbid deceptive legislative practices. Our children must learn the lessons of history. Lest we risk repeating the mistakes of our forebears, we adults must take it upon ourselves right here and right now to reacquaint ourselves with the history lessons we are counting on our children to understand. For it will be our children who will pick up the gauntlet when we are gone and demand that the Constitution be honored and that our politicians conduct all of their affairs with transparency and integrity. If we do our job right and meet our obligations as Americans, it will be everyday citizens who begin the process of restoring integrity, peace, and prosperity. Then it will be up to the parents in America to show our children how to keep it that way.

No Man Is an Angel

Common Sense Conservatives believe the Constitution is a contract between the citizens and the government designed specifically to limit the powers of the government and the majority while protecting the rights of all. Remember that no man is an angel.

There are no angels or philosopher kings on earth,
in business, or in the government.

Where are your political angels? Where are your "government angels" who are pure of heart, pure of mind, and pure of soul? They are at a junket, on TV, at a fund-raiser or "taking care of me and mine."

Therefore, it is never an angel whom we send to Washington to represent us. Progressives often act as though the people cannot be relied upon to make good decisions and, therefore, need the "angels" of government to protect them. Conservatives disagree. As Thomas Jefferson, one of the first Conservatives, said:

Sometimes it is said that man cannot be trusted
with the government of himself. Can he, then, be trusted
with the government of others? Or have we found angels in the form
of kings to govern him? Let history answer this question.

—Thomas Jefferson

The Great Myth

The great myth is that Liberals are for the poor and helpless and that Conservatives are for business and the rich, that employees are necessary and important to our national well-being, but employers are not. Liberals often demonize business interests because they need demons to blame for all things wrong. Conservatives sometimes fall into the trap of defending all things business even though they know that mistakes have been made. Corruption and excessive self-interest at a cost to the people are equal opportunity flaws in character. However, Conservatives tend to base their positions on ensuring equal opportunities and equal treatment for all, along with their perspectives of history, experience, reason, and morality. Whereas Progressives tend to base their opinions on their notion of fairness by using special treatment for some to ensure equal outcomes for all. Their desire to achieve noble objectives at all costs and their emotions get in the way of reason. This dichotomy of equal outcomes versus equal opportunities, special versus equal treatment,

Conservatives want to help the helpless
but not those who can help themselves.

Liberals seem to assume that if you don't believe in their particular
political solutions, then you don't really care about the people that
they claim to want to help. —*Thomas Sowell*

and emotion versus logic often detracts from beneficial communication and principled compromise. Conservatives denounce the
pursuit of noble objectives with flawed means, while Progressives
often claim malevolence whenever there is merely disagreement.

only in governments, but also in businesses, schools, little league baseball, and even playgrounds. *Politics by definition is the process that determines the distribution of wealth and power. What is important is the basis upon which political decisions are made.*

Every two years the American political industry fills the airwaves with the most virulent, scurrilous, wall-to-wall character assassination of nearly every political practitioner in the country—and then declares itself puzzled that America has lost trust in its politicians.

—Charles Krauthammer

If the politics of an organization is based on individual freedoms and the good of society, then the word *politics* describes a virtue. If politics is based on increasing wealth, authority, and power of the politicians or their special interest groups, then the word *politics* describes a vice. We as citizens can decide to participate in the political system that determines how we are governed or we can just be the victims of those who did decide to participate. I am worried about how much power the federal government is accumulating, and I know many other citizens feel the same.

A government that is strong enough to give you everything you want is a government strong enough to take everything you have.

—Winston Churchill

The Constitution is not self-enforcing; it will live on for another generation only if it is alive in the hearts and minds of our children. I keep thinking about this quote:

*All that is necessary for the triumph of evil
is that good men do nothing.*

—Edmund Burke

Freedom Is Never Free

If we don't learn from history, we are doomed to repeat it.

Below is the story I shared with Sammy, my ten-year-old son, in an attempt to explain the process of determining for whom to vote and to provide him with an initial sense of how and where and why Conservatism began.

(July 4, 2009)

Sammy's Story Is the Story of Our Nation's Founding

Once upon a time, the original thirteen states were thirteen British colonies in North America, back when the tales of Captain John Smith, Jamestown, Pocahontas, and even Sir Walter Raleigh were distant memories. It had been more than one hundred years since Western Europeans first settled in the land that became the British Colonies, and those living under British rule in the Colonies were restless. Trouble among the colonists had been growing with increasingly violent and angry outbursts.

The 1600s reflected a time of struggles relating to new settlements such as those in New York and Pennsylvania. The Salem witch trials were held late in the century. By the middle of the 1700s, British rulers were becoming ever more oppressive with the passage of many laws that reduced liberties and raised taxes on the settlers in America, who were still British subjects at the time. The Boston Tea Party in 1773 provided an indication of how out of hand the situation in the colonies had become. This restlessness eventually turned into a rebellion, stemming in large part from high taxes that were imposed on the colonists by the British and the lack of government representation.

The leaders of the colonies tried many times to get the king of England to fix all of the injustices. And when the British ignored their concerns, the Revolutionary War began in April of 1775 at the Battle of Lexington. The "shot heard 'round the world," taken from Ralph Waldo Emerson's "Concord Hymn" in 1837, represented the beginning of the Revolutionary War. A little more than a year later, the thirteen colonies formally separated from Great Britain. They proclaimed their independence from Great Britain in a document called the Declaration of Independence, which was adopted by the Continental Congress on July 4, 1776, and thus formed the original United States of America. This is why Americans call the fourth of July Independence Day.

The British did not take this rebellion lightly, and war continued for about eight years. It took several more years after the war was over for our founding fathers to write and approve the U.S. Constitution, which was in Philadelphia, Pennsylvania, and later ratified by each U.S. state. A constitution is a written body of laws containing principles and rules used to organize a state or a country, and *ratified* means approved.

The short version of this story is that much was accomplished during the twelve-year period ending in 1787. The colonists rebelled against British oppression; declared their independence; established a confederation of states with their first attempt at a constitution; fought and won a long war; and after considerable discussions and negotiations with each other, established the U.S. Constitution that is in existence today.

"Therefore," I said to Sammy, "the official beginning of modern-day Conservatism took place in Philadelphia, Pennsylvania, on September 17, 1787, when the Constitution was signed. And a better answer to the question, 'How do you know who to vote for?' is that you vote for the candidate who is the most capable individual who possesses, supports, and lives by a Common Sense Conservative philosophy."

***

This story was helpful, but I found it was just the beginning. Sammy and his brothers were able to get the general idea that Conservatism was a philosophy of life and politics founded in opposition to government oppression and focused on individual freedoms, but this story alone did not give them a sense of how important this philosophy is today. It also did not convince any of my kids of the need to understand and participate in political matters, nor did it cause them to realize that educating themselves in our history would help them make better decisions in their everyday lives. As an American mom who is proud of her country, I realized that much more needed to be done not only for my boys, but perhaps also for all citizens and all children.

What Do Our Children Know?

I became intrigued and curious as to exactly what my boys really knew about government and how they would (and if they could) answer simple questions about government and governance. In discussing this with my four youngest boys, ages ten to fourteen, only the eldest had a working knowledge of Capitalism, our republic form of government, and the different forms of government in other countries.

At this point, it was clear that each of my boys needed to be educated in these matters. Thus, I began to look for research or curriculum guides to help me begin this educational process. So I searched online booksellers, but I did not find a book written specifically to inform everyday people as to state of the nation and the corrupt nature of our political process. I did not find a book to educate all people in Conservative values that was also designed to help parents educate their kids. There were books with copies of our founding documents, there were a few highly illustrated and narrowly focused children's books on the subject, and there were several highly sophisticated books containing Conservative trea-tises. There were many books on Conservatism, but I found none that I felt really would help me teach my kids what it means to be Conservative and none to help my kids understand why a Conser-vative philosophy is necessary to ensure good governance and to instruct them in life's decisions. What I was looking for was a book titled something such as *Conservatism for Moms and Kids: A Serious Common Sense Guide to Government and Life* by Just A. Mom (who had done her homework), but I did not find it.

What began as a child's question to his mother and the futile search for a comprehensive guide to fully provide the answer sparked the realization that it was incumbent upon me right here and right now to be the mom who wrote that book. When I began, the focus of the book was on providing factual guidance to moms to help them educate their children about Common Sense Conservative values. Just as my sons understood the words in the existing textbooks, which were lacking in the underlying meaning of the concepts, it became clear to me that other parents' children would also be missing the importance of the substance behind the definitions. The more I wrote, the more I came to understand that Sammy's question didn't apply only to me and moms like me—his question and its answer applied to all citizens who deserve a full and meaningful perspective of their place in this country's history and its future.

More Freedom or More Government?

Although our government is based primarily on the balance between individual freedom and limited government, politicians have made government appear complex and hard to understand. Plus, I had not realized how many books were out there criticizing Conservative principles for being too mean spirited and focused on only preserving the rich, while at the same time praising the Liberal philosophy often under the populist guise of fairness, righteousness, hope, social justice, and change. As of late, I have become more and more concerned with the political class on both sides of the aisle. It appeared to me that politicians were getting away with corruption, running up unimaginable debt, and spending fortunes and nearly all of their time running for office, and I believed there were many citizens who felt like I did.

I suspect that most of us need to get up to speed and more involved in nearly all matters political in order to better engage in how our country is being governed and to prepare our kids for that which will surely come their way. For as much as we parents might feel ill equipped or underqualified to materially change the way we are governed or to give our children all of the tools they will need to navigate the jungles we call politics and life, I'm sure we all feel it is our responsibility to do so. We need to get our thoughts in order to be able to properly educate ourselves and our children. Plus, the political system as it stands today is rigged against us, and if we and our kids don't understand and participate in the political system, we could all too easily become victims of it. As I have told my children many times, with hard work and attention to detail, anyone can do nearly anything. I knew I needed to follow my own advice because with hard work and attention to detail, I can do this right here and right now.

ℰℛ

Questions for Kids

1. How do you know whom to vote for?

2. Who has the power and who is in charge: the people or the government?

3. Can regular people make a difference in our country?

4. What are Conservatives trying to conserve?

5. Why is there deception in politics?

6. Why did our founders separate from Great Britain?

7. Who started Conservatism?

8. Why do we have to learn history?

Guiding Thoughts

§

*The trail to American peace and prosperity was
clearly marked by our founding fathers in the
form of individual rights, maximum personal
liberties, and limited governance.*

*No damage has been inflicted on our country or
on our way of life that cannot be repaired with
personal education, broad participation in the
political system, and moral character.*

*The strength of our country resides in the minds
of our children, and the future of our country
will be found in their actions.*

§

§

Right Is Right; Wrong Is Wrong

American Exceptionalism Is Real

Educate and Engage

Children, Patriotism, and Optimism

The Constitution Is a Contract between
Our Government and Its Citizens

It Is Worth Our Effort to Preserve
That which Our Founders Gave Us

The Philosophy of Common Sense Conservatism
Can and Will Prevail

No Man Is an Angel, and It Is Never an Angel
We Send to Washington

Organize Your Thoughts and
Develop Your Own Set of Principles

Think for Yourself and Determine
Your Own Course of Action

We Care, We Are Smart,
and We Can and Will Do This Job Right

America's People are Strong,
and America's Future Remains Bright

§

The Origins and Foundations of Modern Conservatism

(What History Tells Us)

Part One Kids' Page

"Will we do better if we set the prices for a cup of lemonade, the level of sugar in a single ten-ounce drink, and the wages for our workers, or would it be better to let the government do it?"

Mom's and Dad's Mission:

Relate the values, traditions, origins, and principles of modern-day Conservatism.

Kids' Page Summary

The trail to American peace and prosperity was clearly marked by our founding fathers in the form of individual rights, maximum personal liberties, and limited governance. Discover our history and you will discover the foundation of a well-planned and prosperous future for our life, our children, and our country.

The history of Conservatism is important to understanding modern-day Conservative principles, especially what I call Common Sense Conservatism. Our country was founded on principles and notions that were developed not only from an analysis of history and in a quest for freedom, but also in opposition to living under the oppressive hand of Great Britain and the king. Throughout documented history there have been philosophies of freedom that included some level of limitation on government authority. Modern-day Conservatism began on September 17, 1787, when our founding fathers established the U.S. Constitution. On that auspicious day, the individual rights and freedoms given to all by our Creator and expressed in the Declaration of Independence were guaranteed, and tight limits were placed on government authorities. Government was made strong enough to protect us but not so strong as to enable it to take away our liberties.

Conservatives believe in the power and potential of Free-Market Capitalism to provide opportunity for prosperity, to reward individual efforts, and to raise the circumstances of all in society. They further believe in the power and potential of individual people to provide for themselves and their families if given certain freedoms. Freedoms from an overreaching government; of equal justice; from harm, foreign or domestic; and to pursue their own destiny in whatever way they see fit as long as their chosen pursuit does not infringe on the rights of others to do the same are central to this idea.

Conservatism, including its support of Free-Market Capitalism, is more than a political philosophy. It offers a better way to pursue happiness, to govern, and to contribute to society because it is rooted in the tradition of individual freedoms, opportunity, and rights, among which are the right to life, liberty, and the pursuit of happiness. Conservatism provides a set of principles designed to free everyday citizens from the injustice of a potentially oppressive government and maximizes the freedom to pursue personal endeavors of their choice. Common Sense Conservatism adds a focus on children, patriotism, and optimism.

Chapter 1

What a Conservative Believes

W*hat is a person called if he or she believes in the following eighteen principles?*

1. Personal responsibility

2. Moral character

3. Living within one's means

4. Respect for the rule of law

5. Respect for innocent life

6. The importance of limited government

7. Saving for a rainy day

8. The Constitution as a clear, legal document to be interpreted as it was originally written and intended

9. The value of Free-Market Capitalism to all citizens

10. More concern for victims of crime than for the perpetrators of crime

11. The government's primary responsibility to protect its people from harm, foreign or domestic

12. Respect for individual property rights

13. Freedom of religion

14. The right to free speech and free association

15. Punishment that fits the crime

16. An individual's right to enjoy the fruits of his work

17. The freedom to pursue the endeavors of his own choice

18. The responsibility of all men to take care of the truly poor and the needy

People who believe in these eighteen principles are called Conservatives.

History, experience, reason, conscience, and morality tell us what works and what does not. Political philosophies that included ideas and notions of individual freedoms have been around for at least a couple thousand years. However, the foundation of modern-day Conservatism, which grew from these much older historic principles, was fully developed by our founding fathers during the formation of our country. Our founding fathers, in looking for the best form of government for our new nation, were revolutionaries. They built on Western civilization's experience with liberty and democracy and expanded these concepts to include far less government control along with certain individual rights that even the country's leaders could not take away or betray.

Throughout documented history man has mused about individual freedoms and attempted to place limits on government authority. Our founders' study and analysis of the successes and failures of many historical philosophies of life and governance, the principles expressed in the Declaration of Independence, and even such reflections that are in the small book *Common Sense* by Thomas Paine, were great contributors to the notions of

The Constitution is not a self-enforcing document.
It is alive only if it is in the hearts and minds of the people.
The Constitution is a contract between the people and the
government. It protects me from you, you from me,
and me and you from the government.

September 17, 1787: The birth of Conservatism,
a nation of laws, not men.

Conservatism. However, modern-day Conservatism in the United
States formally began September 17, 1787, when the U.S. Constitution was signed. The foundation of modern-day Conservatism was
established with the signing and adoption of the Constitution,
which reaffirmed the values and precepts of the self-evident truths
about human nature and the unalienable rights given to us by our
Creator as set forth in the Declaration of Independence.

Therefore, the original notions and intentions of the Constitution make up the principles that modern-day Conservatives are trying to conserve. The political philosophy of Conservatism combines, in part, individual liberties, restraints on government authority, a republic form of government, Capitalism, a strong defense, and equal application of the rule of law. The life philosophy of Conservatism respects the need for men to be productive, free to pursue their self-interests, moral, personally responsible, self-reliant, and charitable to those in need. Common Sense Conservatism adds a focus on our children, vigorous patriotism, and an optimistic outlook.

The framers of our Constitution meant what they said, and their words were explicit. The founders' intentions were clear that any change made to the Constitution had to be accomplished by constitutional amendment and could not be legitimately instituted by a judge's personal philosophy and/or biased interpretation. We Conservatives believe, as did our founders, in unalienable rights given to us by our Creator that all men are created equal. We are a nation of laws, not a nation of men where birthright or status plays any role in our judicial system.

In reaction to the tyranny of the British monarchy, our founding fathers envisioned and devised a new form of government, which stressed individual freedom consistent with the nature of man while limiting the power of the government and creating what we now know to be a *constitutional republic.* This was a new framework of governance: a nation of laws, not man. Under this system of governance, no king could decide to give favored groups (usually the royalty and those of noble birth) special rights. In a Constitutional Republic, all men are born free. No man or government can take these rights or freedoms without due process and equal application of the law. This concept of Conservatism has stood the test of time based on man's inherent rights.

But our founding fathers knew the country could not exist with merely a conservative political philosophy and constitutional republic form of government. They needed a moral economic system that offered the possibility and potential of prosperity for both individual citizens and society as a whole. They needed an efficient and effective economic system capable of achieving success that could be established within the laws of the land and the moral sensibilities of its people while still protecting the rights of all citizens. In other words, they needed an engine to drive their train of individual liberties and limited government power. That engine was and is Free-Market Capitalism. Together, all four pillars of Conservatism—individual liberties and rights, a constitutional republic, a government of limited authority, and Free-Market Capitalism—provide a moral and efficient economic framework that has given Americans the ability to flourish in great peace and prosperity.

Conservatism is a life and political philosophy that combines individual freedoms with the economic system of Capitalism and a republic form of government within a moral system. Conservatism allows an individual to follow his or her inherent nature to pursue self-interest freely while making significant and material contributions to society as a whole. It does all this while respecting the rights of others to do the same and protecting the rights of all men, without coercion, force, or undue government interference.

Conservatism is not perfect, but it was the preeminent American political philosophy that guided our founding fathers during the successful formation of our government and our nation. Other life and political philosophies that leaned toward more government control and fewer individual liberties have led to other forms of government. All of these other forms of government—Democracy, Communism, Socialism, Monarchy, and Fascism, to name a few—have failed. **Modern-day American Conservatism has, through** *our unique form of American governance, brought the highest standard of living and the most equitable justice for any people in documented history.* Today we hear many of our elected officials emphasize our similarities with other nations around the world. This, in and of itself, is fine. Although we do have many similarities to other nations, it has been our differences that have made our country great.

೧೧

Chapter 2

The Political Balance between Individual Liberties and Government Authority

Tensions between Great Britain and the colonies had been building for more than ten years when the Revolutionary War began at the Battle of Lexington on April 19, 1775. On May 15, 1775, the Second Continental Congress convened with delegates from the thirteen colonies. More than a year later, on July 4, 1776, the Declaration of Independence was signed. After a year of deliberation, our founding fathers developed the Articles of Confederation and Perpetual Union, commonly referred to as the Articles of Confederation. These articles established the first laws of the United States of America and became our first constitution. Our founding fathers, in their initial attempt to limit the tyrannies associated with a too-strong central government, established a too-weak federal government. This government was one that did not have sufficient power to fund itself, to regulate foreign or interstate commerce, or to raise an army to provide needed protections.

U.S. history is exceptional. It was chosen
and founded on freedom from an oppressive government.
It is based on a belief that all people are created equal.

It was in 1787 in Philadelphia that they held another Constitutional Convention to revise the concepts and authorities presented in the Articles of Confederation to grant more power to the federal government to enable it to protect the citizens from harm and still protect the rights of its citizens.

The principles of Conservatism are consistent with historical and permanent elements of human nature going back to the beginning of mankind. There are many "self-evident truths" about human nature. Humans are capable of discerning the difference between good and evil because they are students of history and because they have reasoning and consciences. The statement that these truths are self-evident means these beliefs and principles are obvious to all and known to be true through hundreds of years of observation. In other words, the very nature of these truths is such that they are undeniable and clear without needing additional proof.

Every person has unalienable rights given to us by our Creator, among which is that everyone is born free and equal. Men and women know right from wrong, but our founders knew that this fact alone would not be enough to ensure that men and women would necessarily follow only their better instincts. Human nature has its vices and virtues. Mankind is naturally geared for survival and self-interest.

Human nature presents a paradox: man can be greedy and ambitious but can also be generous and caring. The founders of our country seemed to have a very good grasp on the nature of man when they wrote the Constitution and structured our government. The Constitution and laws of the land were set not only to protect certain rights, but they were also focused on controlling the lesser instincts and the common vices of man. The extensive set of constitutional checks and balances along with the laws that called for proportionate punishment for crimes committed revealed that our founders recognized that when man accumulates too much power, corruption and abuse soon follow; when man is left fully unchecked, criminal behavior is too often the result.

The founders relied on the strength of character found in so many men and women, the power of the philosophy of good contained in spirituality, the potential rewards of Capitalism, and the fear of punishment for unjust behavior to bring out the virtue in men.

The U.S. Constitution reflects the founders' understanding that some limited amount of freedom needed to be given up to empower a central government to make it capable of providing certain necessary protections and services. However, they had just fought and won a war with an overreaching monarchy. They endured this great sacrifice of wealth and life because they had experienced firsthand the oppression of an overbearing government. Therefore, they were determined to limit the reach and authority of their new government.

In framing a government which is to be administered
by men over men, the great difficulty lies in this:
you must first enable the government to control the governed;
and in the next place oblige it to control itself.

—James Madison (suspected author),
The Federalist Papers, No. 51

The addition of the economic system of Capitalism to the existing individual freedoms and the limitations on central governance provided economic incentives consistent with man's natural tendency to pursue self-interest while also contributing to his community. All that was left was for good people to function within the framework of the Constitution to reap the potential rewards offered through Free-Market Capitalism and to engage in the political process that allowed them a say in the way they would be governed.

Chapter 3

Capitalism: Origin and Foundation of the Economic System of Conservatism

Conservatism is a life and political philosophy consistent with human nature, limited government, and unalienable rights for individuals. But in order for Conservatism to work, it requires a moral and efficient economic system that also is consistent with human nature and the general needs of society. That system is Free-Market Capitalism. Capitalism is the vehicle that offers the potential for prosperity not just for the individual, but also for all of society. Just as a rising tide raises all ships, Free-Market Capitalism has the potential to improve the circumstances of all people.

Adam Smith was a Scottish moral philosopher and a pioneer of political economics. His seminal book on Capitalism, *An Inquiry into the Nature and Causes of the Wealth of Nations*, commonly known as *The Wealth of Nations*, was published in 1776 and had great impact on American commerce and society. Adam Smith spoke often of the value of free markets.

Capitalism Equals Opportunity: Master of Your Fate

*Every individual . . . generally, indeed, neither intends to
promote the public interest, nor knows how much he is promoting it.
By preferring the support of domestic to that of foreign industry he
intends only his own security; and by directing that industry in such
a manner as its produce may be of the greatest value, he intends only
his own gain, and he is in this, as in many other cases, led by an
invisible hand to promote an end which was no part of his intention.*

—The Wealth of Nations, Book IV, Chapter II

*Man has almost constant occasion for the help of his brethren,
and it is in vain for him to expect it from their benevolence only.*

—The Wealth of Nations, Book I, Chapter I

*The property which every man has in his own labour, as it is the
original foundation of all other property, so it is the most sacred and
inviolable. The patrimony of a poor man lies in the strength and
dexterity of his hands; and to hinder him from employing this strength
and dexterity in what manner he thinks proper without injury to his
neighbour, is a plain violation of this most sacred property.*

—The Wealth of Nations, Book I, Chapter X, Part II

Capitalism, as Adam Smith wrote in *The Wealth of Nations*, is driven by an element of human nature he described as "self-interest." Smith held the view that it was in a baker's self-interest to bake the best loaf of bread possible and to offer that bread at the most competitive price possible. He felt that this approach to commerce would create demand for the bread and allow both buyer and seller to benefit. Thus the baker could provide for himself and his family while providing a needed and wanted product for others in his community. Free-Market Capitalism allows this method to be performed repeatedly by everyone from blacksmiths to lawyers.

Free-Market Capitalism allows an individual to fulfill him- or herself as a human being by offering the potential to each citizen to become fully self-actualized. It offers the opportunity for every citizen to feel individual pride, to be rewarded fairly for his efforts, and to have incentives to do good work. It also provides incentive for individuals to innovate to improve products and services, which has the potential to benefit not only themselves, but once again, all of society. Capitalism offers an equal opportunity to individuals to take advantage of their own ingenuity and hard work and to enjoy the fruits of their labor.

Adam Smith recognized the need to provide an economic system that offered the opportunity for individuals to personally prosper from their own efforts. At the same time, the nature of this economic system also needed those same individual efforts to contribute to the betterment of society, irrespective of the individual's intent or desire to make those contributions.

As Adam Smith stated, the invisible hand of free markets allowed society to benefit because the buyers' and sellers' transactions provided benefits not just to themselves, but also to all of society. A baker's making loaves that others will want to buy gives the baker the incentive to continue making the best loaf of bread he can so he can maximize his own rewards. The buyers will get a great loaf of bread, and the baker will have money to buy other goods and services at fair-trade prices. The more people who like and buy the baker's bread, the more people the baker can hire. The more jobs the baker provides, the greater the increase in societal commerce and wealth.

When You Don't Have Capitalism

When you don't have Capitalism (which might better be described as Free-Market Capitalism), you have government-central planning. In place of prices and wages being determined by millions of people making billions of independent transactions based on supply and demand or their own individual criteria, without Free-Market Capitalism, there would be government elitists (central planners) determining wages and prices.

The question is whether one believes that individual economic self-interest is superior or inferior to elitist's political self-interest.

The answer to this question has been demonstrated throughout recorded history in locations around the world. The economic self-interest of Free-Market Capitalism offers superior results to individuals, to government, and to society as a whole (including those who are poor or in despair).

Markets are a long way from perfect, but central planners are far less fair, accurate, and productive. With central planning almost all incentive to innovate and improve is erased. The built-in incentives of Free-Market Capitalism create the prosperity and productivity that funds individual enterprises, raises societal living standards, defends the country, and provides a safety net for those in need.

The outcome of commerce in our nation is not guaranteed. The millions of sellers and buyers who make billions of decisions every day determine the outcomes. Conservatism allows our nation's laws and the independent dictates of our free marketplace to provide the guideposts to fairness. Our Constitution and Capitalist ways offer a moral system that, by law, has to give everyone equal opportunity for life, liberty, and the pursuit of happiness.

☙❧

The Wizard of Id by Brant Parker and Johnny Hart

☙❧

Chapter 4

Constitutional Republic
versus Democracy

America was founded on the principle of elected individuals representing the people in the form of a constitutional republic, not a democracy. In a constitutional republic, the government is bound by a written constitution designed, among other things, to protect individual rights. Over the centuries democracies have come and gone. All failed in large part because of their lack of moral foundation and their lack of protection of the equal rights of all men, which often resulted in the oppression of minorities. Respect for individual liberty and protection of equal rights for everyone are at the very foundation of Conservatism and America's greatness.

After winning independence in the Revolutionary War, our founding fathers were able to choose and create a new government for the new United States. While some leaders wanted George Washington to be king, our founding fathers were great students of history and did not want to repeat past failures. They did not want another oppressive government after they had just fought so hard to be free from one.

*A free people [claim] their rights as derived from the laws of nature,
and not as the gift of their chief magistrate.*

—Thomas Jefferson

Our founding fathers' philosophy was to have a government
based on laws, not on the whims and notions of a king or a few rich
and powerful people. Many forms of government were ruled out
because of their absolute government controls and their restriction
on individual liberties. The only options left for consideration were
a republic or a democracy. In a pure democracy, a majority rules
absolutely and without constraints, and the minority has no rights
or protections from the emotional or populist whims and notions
of the majority. Absolute rule by any group poses obvious potential
problems as noted by Thomas Jefferson.

*A democracy is nothing more than mob rule, where fifty-one percent
of the people may take away the rights of the other forty-nine.*

—Thomas Jefferson

A constitutional republic form of government represented the
basic philosophy of our founding fathers to have a government
strong enough to protect our country, its citizens, and our rights
from all enemies, but not a government so strong as to be oppressive
or able to diminish our rights and our freedoms.

Many people confuse a republic with a democracy. These two
different forms of government are often seen as being the same or
at least very similar. The United States of America is too often
referred to as a democracy. One suspects this is done, in part,

because it creates a good populist sound bite. But it could also be because the advantages and protections of a constitutional republic (that do not exist in a pure democracy) are not entirely understood by a large segment of people in America. Certainly a constitutional republic has its democratic elements (e.g., one man, one vote; regular elections; government power derived from the people). However, our founders recognized the potential tyranny of a pure democracy and put in place the protections of a constitutional republic, which protects all citizens' rights and freedoms with constitutional rules and authorities. The founding fathers were very aware of the pitfalls and dangers of a pure democracy based on the caprices of a simple majority versus a constitutional republic based on unchanging rights, obligations, and liberties.

An anecdote often attributed to Benjamin Franklin, but in dispute as to its origin(s), is still quite apt here:

"Democracy is two wolves and a lamb voting on what to have for lunch. Liberty is a well-armed lamb contesting the vote."

—Benjamin Franklin

Our founders were clear on the necessity of a constitutional republic that included a set of laws and regulations written with the specific intent to overrule the potentially unjust passions of the majority whenever those passions transgressed on another citizen's rights and freedoms.

Our American republic is based on two important founding documents, the Constitution and the Declaration of Independence. In neither of these documents does the word *democracy* appear—not even once.

"Democracy is two wolves and a lamb voting on what to have for lunch. Liberty is a well-armed lamb contesting the vote."

The United States Is a Constitutional Republic

Remember democracy never lasts long.
It soon wastes, exhausts, and murders itself. There never was
a democracy yet that did not commit suicide.

—John Adams

The majority, oppressing an individual,
is guilty of a crime, abuses its strength, and by acting on the law
of the strongest breaks up the foundations of society.

—Thomas Jefferson

Government is instituted for the common good;
for the protection, safety, prosperity, and happiness of the people;
and not for profit, honor, or private interest of any one man, family,
or class of men; therefore, the people alone have an incontestable,
unalienable, and indefeasible right to institute government;
and to reform, alter, or totally change the same, when their
protection, safety, prosperity, and happiness require it.

—John Adams, Thoughts on Government, 1776

☙

Chapter 5

Conservatism: A Moral System of Rules and Laws

*D*eclaration of Independence. A key part of our founding documents is the Declaration of Independence signed July 4, 1776, in Philadelphia, Pennsylvania. This document referenced what our founding fathers felt were the self-evident truths and natural rights of all people.

The Declaration of Independence offered the formal justification for the original thirteen colonies to declare their independence from Great Britain. Our founding fathers declared the United States to be a new and free nation. They laid the moral foundation and political philosophy for the establishment of a new nation with a government that could and would provide for the safety of and equal opportunity for all of its citizens. Our founders further declared that it was not only their right to throw off the despotic government of Great Britain, but also their duty.

To further understand the importance of these documents and how revolutionary they were, one must understand the harsh and difficult times in which our founding fathers were living. For more than ten years before July of 1776, while the people were still under British rule, among other tyrannies, the settlers endured high taxation and regulation without any say in how they were being governed. In spite of these chronic injustices, neither our founders nor the other colonists took this separation from Great Britain lightly. They diligently pursued and repeatedly petitioned for redress of their grievances through the appropriate British channels of communication of the time. However, each petition for remedy was met with further injury from the king. The colonists warned the king and his officials again and again of the consequences of continued despotism and tyranny by Great Britain, but their warnings fell on deaf ears. Finally, when the British abuses increased and when the colonial patriots who participated in the Second Continental Congress were declared

The Declaration of Independence is the moral foundation of our nation: every man is free and equal

traitors to Great Britain, the colonists accepted the unwelcome truth that their appeals for justice would never be honored.

On April 19, 1775, the Revolutionary War began with the Battle of Lexington in Massachusetts, and within about a year, the Continental Congress of the Thirteen Colonies unanimously declared their separation from the rule of Great Britain in the Declaration of Independence.

The Continental Congress, led by our American founding fathers John Adams, Benjamin Franklin, George Washington, James Madison, Alexander Hamilton, John Jay, and Thomas Jefferson, among others, formed a committee to draft the Declaration of Independence. Jefferson did most of the initial drafting and was specifically responsible for the inclusion of the expanded rights of people and the limited role of government. Today this document continues to serve as notice to all nations of the birth of a new nation. *On July 4, 1776, the United States of America became its own country.*

The settlers of the new United States of America endured eight years of costly fighting for the ideals our founding fathers had laid out in the Declaration of Independence. Many lives, much wealth, and substantial property were lost during this fight for independence. The Revolutionary War proved beyond a doubt that freedom does not come without substantial cost. We learned from our founding fathers and the many citizen freedom fighters of the Revolutionary War era a fact that is still evident: freedom is not free.

The Declaration of Independence was important not only because it justified the independence of the colonists by listing the grievances thrust upon the colonists by the unfair British rule, but also because it provided a fair and just political philosophy that would be used in the formation of a new government to support the founding of a new nation. The Declaration of Independence was also used as a tool to explain to all colonists the necessary and urgent need for the colonies to separate from Great Britain. In simple terms, it was used to convince the general population and the officials of each separate colony of the necessity to band together and join the fight for independence.

The founders outlined the moral vision of a philosophy of government based on natural law and provided a compelling argument for breaking their allegiance to and freeing themselves from the king. Although it accomplished many objectives, it was most important to declare and clearly state four key facts and beliefs:

1. *"We hold these truths to be self-evident, that all men are created equal, that they are endowed by their Creator with certain unalienable Rights, that among these are Life, Liberty, and the pursuit of Happiness."* Notwithstanding the initial material flaws represented by slavery and limited women's rights (which were eventually corrected), this meant that all men were born free and created equal; therefore, their freedom was not challengeable without due process, and each person had the right to be treated equally under the law regardless of his station in life. It further meant that this freedom was not a gift from any government or bestowal from any man, but that the rights to be free and equal were gifts that came directly to each person from man's Creator.

2. It itemized the king's "history of repeated injuries and usurpations" and the many unaddressed and unremedied abuses and injustices committed against the colonists by Great Britain.

3. It pointed out the colonists' firm belief that governments derived their just powers only from the consent of those being governed. This statement reflected the notion that men are not born into power and that a just government does

not have unlimited rights to rule over its people. It further suggested that the people deserve to have a say (including final approval) in the way they would be governed.

4. By the authority of the people of the colonies, the thirteen states were then independent states, separated from Great Britain, absolved of any prior allegiance to the Crown; all political connections between the colonies and Great Britain were and ought to have been dissolved. It further declared that as free and independent states, they would now have the right to conduct their own affairs in a fashion similar to that of any other independent nation.

The first sentences of the Declaration of Independence acknowledged the colonists' beliefs that people are free by nature's God, irrespective of the traditions of birthright.

When in the course of human events, it becomes necessary for one people to dissolve the political bands which have connected them with another, and to assume among the powers of the earth, the separate and equal station to which the laws of nature and of nature's God entitle them, a decent respect to the opinions of mankind requires that they should declare the causes which impel them to the separation.

—Declaration of Independence

Moreover, these famous first few lines justified the actions of the founders and reflected the political principles, rights, ideas, and the founders' vision for the new nation.

The document further implies that moral law, instituted and established by the consent of the people, is superior to government law, established by a few elites, in part because it is based not only on political will, but also on the God-given unalienable rights of individuals and on reason. It is reason and higher law that create the moral foundation of our political system.

The Declaration of Independence treats all citizens equally, but it does not say everyone is created with equal ability or is guaranteed equal rewards for their efforts; it provides only for equal opportunity. That is, not all people have equal ability to play violin or baseball, and neither has the right to be successful at such matters as music or sports. Each has only the equal right to seek their opportunity or desire as long as they respect and do not infringe on the rights of others to do the same.

⊗ℐ

Chapter 6

The U.S. Constitution

After winning independence, the need for a new plan to govern a new nation was necessary, thus the U.S. Constitution was born. In 1787 a new set of constitutional laws and guidelines were established. Together, the Declaration of Independence and the Constitution are considered key founding documents of our country. The Constitution, drafted upon the principles our founding fathers had outlined in the Declaration of Independence, is the supreme law of the land. James Madison is considered to have been a driving force and the primary drafter of the Constitution.

The Constitution offers a moral philosophy that provides for individual freedoms and a social outlook that stresses independence, trust in U.S. citizens, and self-reliance. The Constitution protects citizens from an overreaching government and the potential of an overzealous or emotional majority while securing certain individual rights, including the rights to bear arms, be free from unreasonable search and seizure, free speech, and freedom of religion. The government derives its limited powers from the people. The federal government is given only those powers it requires to do that which

The government works for the people;
the people do not work for the government.

can better be accomplished at the federal (as opposed to the state or personal) level. These limited powers were designed to enable the federal government to carry out such responsibilities as to protect its citizens, to facilitate interstate commerce, and to create an environment of domestic tranquility and equal opportunity. *The government works for the people; the people do not work for the government.*

The government is designed with a separation of powers, or a system of checks and balances, developed with the specific intent that none of the three branches of government (the executive, the judicial, or the legislative) could become too strong or dominant. A primary purpose of the Constitution is to limit the power of government. The founders' mission was to devise a government that would protect us from our enemies, whether the enemies are foreign or domestic.

Obviously the people granted only certain powers to the government. These powers were enumerated, meaning the Constitution contained a listing of federal authorities and prohibitions. All rights and powers not enumerated were reserved for the states and their citizens. The final responsibility to see that the Constitution is upheld remains in the hands of the people.

In the first place it is to be remembered that the general government is not to be charged with the whole power of making and administering laws. Its jurisdiction is limited to certain enumerated objects, which concern all the members of the republic, but which are not to be attained by the separate provisions of any.

—James Madison (suspected author),
The Federalist Papers, No. 14

The founders crafted and approved the Bill of Rights to further protect and clarify certain individual rights and to guard against what they felt might be the tendency for the federal government to expand its powers beyond that which was originally intended and authorized. Subsequently, seventeen additional constitutional amendments were approved by the Congress and ratified by the states.

*A Bill of Rights is what the people are entitled to
against every government, and what no just government
should refuse, or rest on inference.*

—Thomas Jefferson

The Constitution makes crystal clear the rights of the people and the limitations of the majority and the federal government. Both are carefully and meticulously spelled out. Rights are rights, which go well beyond the notion of privileges. More important, however, is that privileges are not rights.

☙❧

Chapter 7

Conservatism: Optimistic on Life

J ust as the founders of the United States wanted to ensure their freedoms in 1787 and for their posterity, so do Conservatives today. Conservatism seeks to minimize the tax and regulatory burden on citizens and businesses. Conservatism is not antigovernment; it is simply against excessive government. It sees a legitimate need for limited responsibilities and authorities of government, while it also recognizes the inherent inefficiency of government operations. Among other things, it recognizes that more government often equals less individual freedom. Conservatives believe it is human nature to pursue self-interest, to take pride in individual accomplishment, to seek self-reliance, and to embrace personal responsibility and accountability for family and community. However, Conservatives are also aware of the flaws in some men. Therefore, Conservatives also support swift and fair law enforcement.

Conservatives believe that in most circumstances, individuals can fend for and take care of themselves if provided the freedoms of equal opportunity, of equal justice, from the tyranny of an overreaching government, from harm both domestic and foreign (domestic tranquility), and to choose their own path to prosperity and happiness. In other words, Conservatives believe that these characteristics of people are natural, right, permanent, and unchanging throughout the generations; given equal and guaranteed opportunity for life, liberty, and the pursuit of happiness, people can do well on their own. These Conservative beliefs in self-reliance are not, however, an argument for ignoring the needs of those who are infirm, victims of natural disasters or terrorism, or otherwise unable to take care of themselves through no fault of their own. To the contrary, Conservatives support government and private assistance for those truly in need but are against making our citizens unnecessarily dependent on government or private assistance.

Conservatives support the notion that success and achievement are positive virtues to be rewarded and celebrated because individual success is the force that raises the economic tide and, therefore, has the potential to raise the circumstances of all in our society. History, experience, reason, and morality have taught us that no political and economic system other than Free-Market Capitalism exercised within the structure of a constitutional republic has ever raised so many individuals out of poverty and despair. Conservatism, including its key economic driver, Free-Market Capitalism, simply offers a better way to live, a better way to pursue self-interest, and a better way to contribute to society because it is rooted in tradition of individual freedom and equal opportunity for all.

Purpose of Parables

Below is the first of six parables that present a running story in a lemonade stand setting designed to help children better understand and learn important principles of life, politics, and governance. Each is designed to show how a particular principle applies to everyday life. Why parables? Because they offer a moral lesson that kids can understand of how Common Sense Conservative principles affect them every day.

Parable #1

"Trouble at the Lemonade Stand"

There's a place called Liberty, where the people are friendly and happy and helpful. All kinds of folk live here—tall, short, young, old, skinny, not, you name it—and mostly they get along just fine. This story is about five of them, five young friends named Tommy, John, Benny, Roger, and Robbie.

One summer day, when the weather was hot and dry and everybody was thirsty, Tommy said to his friends, "We should build a lemonade stand. It'd help people cool off in this heat, and we could make a little money too."

Well, John, Benny, Roger, and Robbie thought this was an awesome idea, so they gathered up some wood, nails, hammers, and saws and they got busy. After a lot of hard work, sweat, and smashed thumbs, the kids were done. Maybe their lemonade stand wasn't the prettiest thing you ever saw, but they'd made it with their own hands, and they were proud of it. They hurried home and mixed up a few gallons of lemonade, and soon they were open for business.

That lemonade was good and cold and just what everybody wanted on a hot summer day. The kids' stand was a big success . . . at least till Georgie found out about it.

Now you have to understand one thing. Ol' Georgie King was not a nice kid. In a town full of friendly, happy, helpful people, this fellow was unfriendly and unhappy and unhelpful. He was just a plain old brat and a bully too. "Look, you kids," ol' Georgie growled at Tommy and his friends. "I don't want a lemonade stand on my block unless it's *my* lemonade stand. You unnerstand?"

Well, the last thing these kids wanted was trouble. So they packed up and moved down a block. It was a lot of hot, sweaty work, but once again their lemonade stand was a hit. In fact, it was an even bigger hit than before. I can't tell you how many gallons they sold, but everybody who tasted it said it was the best lemonade they'd ever had.

Of course it wasn't long before Georgie found out about the new place. This time he made a bargain with the kids. "Look, you kids. Here's the deal. You pay me a chunk of what you make, an' I'll be sure nobody bothers you. That's the deal; take it or leave it. You unnerstand?"

Well, Tommy, John, Benny, Roger, and Robbie talked it over. They didn't like Georgie's plan—no sirree, didn't like it one bit—but they decided they'd go along with it. It was better than packing up and moving again.

"All right, Georgie," said Tommy. "We'll take your deal."

The summer days kept rolling by, and the good folk of Liberty kept buying lemonade from Tommy and his friends. And the kids kept paying Georgie a chunk of it. But the more lemonade they sold, the more money Georgie wanted. He even sent some bully pals to make sure the kids paid on time.

Finally, Tommy and his friends had had enough. They were fed up, they were tired of getting bullied. So they talked it over and decided not to pay anymore.

Next time Georgie came by for his money, Tommy said, "No."

"Say what?" said Georgie.

"We said no," answered John.

"We don't like your deal," added Benny. "You keep changing it, and that isn't fair."

"Whoa, whoa, whoa!" shouted Georgie. "You can't talk to me like that!"

And that's when Roger poured out the whole pitcher of lemonade, right there on the sidewalk. All of it. Every drop.

"Hey, hey, hey!" screamed Georgie. "What do you think you're doing?"

"We'd rather dump it than pay you," said Robbie.

Well, Georgie didn't know what to say. He stormed off and the kids weren't sure what he'd do next. But they knew one thing: they had stood up to the bully, and it felt good.

The moral of the story: Freedom is never free. Defend it or lose it.

It was wrong to make the kids pay Georgie. Tommy and his friends were standing up for what's right. They made it clear that they wouldn't take his bullying anymore.

Note to parents: This is an allegory for the United States and its relation with Great Britain's King George III. The Declaration and Resolves of the First Continental Congress of 1774 led to the Revolutionary War of 1775–1787 and to the ratification of the Declaration of Independence in 1776.

Questions for Kids

Part I—Questions Kids Ask

1. What have we learned from history?

2. How do Conservatives help the poor and needy?

3. Who was Adam Smith, and what did he do?

4. Should I be a Republican or a Democrat?

5. Do we have a democracy in America?

6. Where do our rights come from?

7. What truths are held as self-evident and why?

8. What is the Bill of Rights?

9. What makes our country different from other countries?

10. How do you know whom to vote for in elections?

11. How do regular people make a difference in our country?

12. What are conservatives trying to conserve?

Part Two

Eleven Conservative Principles

Part Two Kids' Page

"Who will keep us safe? Who will protect us from crime? How can we defend ourselves? What will help us be successful, and can we find success on our own while still being fair to others?"

Mom's and Dad's Mission:

Relate the eleven key Conservative principles supported by our founding fathers, the Declaration of Independence, and the U.S. Constitution.

Kids' Page Summary

The purpose of having principles and theories is to help organize thought, and the ultimate purpose of organized thought is to help in deciding a course of action. These eleven Conservative principles are designed to keep us safe, provide an opportunity for all citizens to prosper, support individual rights and freedoms, keep government in its place, and define moral character. Part II takes Conservative theory and converts it to specific Conservative principles that will help us take back our country, right here and right now. These principles are, in fact, what we have learned from history, experience, reason, conscience, and morality.

The first three principles relating to strong defense, domestic tranquility (keep our neighborhoods safe), and self-defense are necessary to protect us from our foreign enemies and from home-grown criminals. Keeping the country safe is the first responsibility of government. The next four principles relate to providing opportunity and the potential for each citizen to earn his or her way into prosperity. Capitalism, property rights, free trade, and fiscal responsibility (spending wisely) all help to create an atmosphere that allows people the chance for personal and business success. The next two principles of limited government and individual responsibility are two sides of the same coin.

A certain level of government is necessary to do that which cannot be done or done well at the state or citizen level (e.g., raise an army and regulate interstate commerce). However, the more power given to government, the fewer rights for individuals. Finding the right balance between necessary government authority and individual liberty is the issue. The last two principles are about personal accountability and individual conduct. Our nation was founded on the concepts of personal responsibility, self-reliance, and moral character.

Common Sense Conservatism requires us to develop practical principles that can be applied to everyday circumstances in life and in politics. These eleven principles will help us to make decisions that will benefit our children, to see the good in our country, and to perform actions that will justify our general optimism. It is these eleven principles and the power of *we the people* that are the keys to taking back our country, right here and right now.

Chapter 8

The Three Levels of Protection for a Peaceful and Free Society

Principle 1: Strong Defense
Principle 2: Ensure Domestic Tranquility
Principle 3: The Right to Self-defense

We have learned from history, experience, reason, conscience, and morality that for a nation to have a free, prosperous, and peaceful society, there must be certain citizen and property protections. This knowledge exists in our institutional memory. We as individuals must rediscover that which our founding fathers brought to light and documented for us. We need to rediscover it right here and right now.

In writing the Constitution, the intent of our founding fathers included securing individual liberties by limiting the power and reach of the government, placing limits and restrictions on the majority, establishing unalienable rights for every citizen, and promoting strong foundations for a positive social order for all and their posterity. But they also had to establish a government strong enough to allow it to ensure domestic tranquility and to protect the country from foreign and domestic harm. In order for citizens to exercise their rights and pursue their individual interests, they first need to be free from terrorists, nation-state enemies, mob rule, and domestic criminals.

All of the many rights and freedoms that are envisioned and documented in the Declaration of Independence and the Constitution assume a free society conducting its affairs in a safe and secure country. Therefore, an initial and primary responsibility of government is to protect its country and, by extension, its people. The Preamble of the Constitution guarantees that the federal government will (and therefore, must) *"provide for the common defense."*

Therefore, the Three Levels of Protection:

Strong Defense: The purpose of the military and our foreign intelligence agencies is to protect our country and its citizens from foreign enemies and to project a power so strong as to discourage so much as consideration of an attack on our country.

Ensure Domestic Tranquility: A combination of professional domestic law enforcement, the rule of law, and an unbiased judiciary provide the second level of protection. Our courts and law-enforcement agencies need the capacity and the legal authority to coordinate with each other at the federal, state, and local levels. Domestic law-enforcement agencies need to meet their obligation to protect people's rights and to catch and detain criminals in a manner consistent with the laws of the land. Criminals and potential criminals need to sense a strong likelihood that they will be identified, captured, and punished if they commit an offense. To be effective, the judiciary needs to conduct its matters such that it develops a reputation for being fair and impartial and for meting out punishment that fits the crime: the greater or lesser the consequences of the crime, the greater or lesser the punishment. The individual rights guaranteed by our Constitution and the laws of the land also need to protect the minority from the whims of the majority.

The Right to Self-defense (including the right to bear arms provided in the Second Amendment): Citizens have the Constitutional right to protect and defend themselves, their family, and their property. This right exists to allow individuals some capacity to personally defend themselves by providing both a psychological and physical barrier from criminals. There are three other reasons for its being included: (1) to enable civilians to help (if needed) in case of foreign attack, (2) to protect ourselves from an unruly and unreasonable majority, and (3) to enable individuals to protect themselves from their own government should some part of that government become tyrannical, overreaching, and nonresponsive to constitutional checks and balances or administrative appeals for redress.

Principle 1: Strong Defense

Principle 1: Strong Defense—Peace through Strength. The purpose of the military is to protect our country and our citizens from foreign enemies, so we may live in peace.

Better be despised for too anxious apprehensions,
than ruined by too confident security.

—Edmund Burke

The very first priority of Conservatism is the government's number one responsibility: to protect the people from all enemies foreign and domestic. This truth is self-evident. If we do not have a safe and sovereign country, nothing else matters. If the people are not safe in their homes, they are not free. Without security, there would be no debating over politics, prices, or other matters; there would be no freedom. Without security, there would be only death, enslavement, and tyranny. Without security, all that the patriots escaped from in 1776 would be lost.

The principle of strong defense demands the government take appropriate steps to protect the people from harm with a very powerful military, a proficient intelligence network, and the latest weapons and equipment technology. America has the most envied and the most powerful military in the world, which is now served by people who willingly enlist. Gone are the compulsory service, draft dodgers, and conscientious objectors of a few decades ago. Our defense begins with a strong navy, army, air force, Marines, Coast Guard, National Guard, and CIA, among many other agencies, all of which report to civilian authority. The Department of Defense is responsible for maintaining a trained and well-equipped

Peace through Strength: Don't Take My Lemonade Stand

Walk Softly and Carry a Big Stick

fighting force, supporting current operations, and being prepared for future operations. As part of our balance of powers, the secretary of defense is a civilian, as is the commander in chief, our president.

Theodore Roosevelt, the twenty-sixth president of the United States, commented on America's foreign policy in saying, **"Speak softly and carry a big stick."** That is, our country needs to be respectful in its communications and to use diplomacy where possible but to have a powerful military both as a deterrent and as a final option. Conservatives are often very suspicious and critical of Liberals and others who might want to lessen the size and capability of our military or reduce our defense capability. The meek might inherit the Earth, but only after they have been conquered and put into servitude.

Conservatives believe that much can be accomplished through diplomatic relations but are well aware that military weakness invites trouble. Conservatives also recognize that many regimes are reasonable and, therefore, subject to fair negotiations and logical debate. But Conservatives also understand that many tyrants use diplomacy and rational-sounding discussions as a weapon to buy time to prepare for more aggressive and destructive actions. Conservatives know that these tyrants respond positively to diplomatic discussion only when the nation they are talking to has demonstrated overwhelming power and the courage and commitment to use this power if necessary.

Peace through strength:

You have enemies? Good. That means you've stood up for something, sometime in your life.

—Winston Churchill

Strong defense is an integral part of our foreign policy. A strong defense and a powerful military are often the unused tools that allow us to resolve our serious differences with rogue nations through peaceful means. Conservatives believe that this is no time to abandon our strategy of peace through strength, and it is no time to forget history or the evils that lie in some men.

Of the four wars in my lifetime,
none came about because the U.S. was too strong.

—Ronald Reagan

Peace is not the absence of conflict; it is the ability
to handle conflict by peaceful means.

—Ronald Reagan

In the past the geographical boundaries of the United States afforded some protection from foreign attack. For a long while, the Pacific and Atlantic oceans provided barriers from aggressors from the east and west; and our generally friendly neighbors of Canada and Mexico provided some additional buffer zones both north and south. However, in the past sixty or seventy years, advancements in weapons and their delivery systems have nearly eliminated these safe barriers. Many of our enemies (and one-time enemies) now have the capability to annihilate millions of Americans with just one nuclear bomb. And despite the perceptions of some Liberals, many others are on the path to develop and perhaps use these weapons of mass destruction.

The strength of America's foreign policy and America's might is essential not only to Americans, but also to all peaceful and free people throughout the world. The world is a dangerous place, and there is much evil in the world that understands only the language of power and the potential of a nearly impenetrable defense and a crushing retaliation. Conservatives know that America is the prime target for nearly all enemies of freedom, and in many cases, America stands as the only impediment to rogue nations and terrorists who wish to conquer, rule, and oppress.

Much of the world depends on America's goodness and her military to meet the injustices of rogue nations that often trade in genocide, hunger, repression, and human suffering. Regardless of noisy criticisms, the world looks to America to stabilize the international financial markets, to eliminate or reduce terrible threats, and to promote economic growth at home and around the world. As America goes, so goes the world.

What would happen if America abandoned its "peace through strength" strategy?

What would occur if America followed the Liberal and often pacifist idea of reducing its commitment to defense and the military? What if those who labor under the misapprehension that the world is no longer a dangerous place or who feel more money should be put into domestic welfare programs were able to sway this national policy? In other words, what if the defense of our country became secondary in importance to local or regional concerns? The answer could well be devastating.

Conservatives believe that America needs weapons systems and troops to defend us from the oft-stated threats coming from such countries as North Korea and Iran. America needs military funding and political support to maintain the fights and assure victory in places such as Afghanistan and to maintain our hard-fought and costly gains in countries such as Iraq. Conservatives believe that America must prepare for the major threats of missile attacks with antimissile systems to defend us from nations that think and act like North Korea or Iran. Conservatives believe that the United States must address and be prepared to defend the potential threat of an ever-growing naval buildup in China or the reemergence of Russia's military aircraft.

Conservatives are worried that even a short-lived (one or two presidential terms) Liberal "weak on defense" strategy could irreparably harm America's defense contractor infrastructure and cause America to lose specialized factories along with highly skilled and capable workers who are essential to keep our national defense strong. Loss of our defense industry would have a tragic economic impact and potentially devastating national security consequences. Even if our country could survive such an unraveling of capabilities, replacing these individuals and this infrastructure would be difficult and time consuming, laying us bare to further attack.

Reduced support of the military leads to a hollow force. For example, in the recent deployments in Afghanistan and Iraq, the United States has had to scramble to deploy enough units; call back to active duty a substantial number of National Guard soldiers; and extend many regular army, navy, air force, and Marine deployments. The Liberal answer to this situation seems to be that we could compensate for a weakened military structure with better public relations and a bigger and better diplomatic corps. There is the constant need to update and modernize the military. If we do not invest in defense, our defense will become outmoded, weakened, and eventually compromised.

If our country is seen as weak, threats will quickly emerge. History has taught us what happens when there is no resolve and no muscle behind foreign policy. There were likely many other factors, but it seems more than obvious that during President Jimmy Carter's era, Russia invaded Afghanistan and the Iranian

Islamic extremists seized American hostages. It did not go unnoticed that when Ronald Reagan took office, our hostages were released immediately, and it wasn't long before the Soviet Union left Afghanistan and ultimately disintegrated. A Conservative reputation has its advantages.

Today certain Islamic countries such as Iran and Syria, along with the totalitarian Communist country of North Korea are seriously dangerous. Each has intent to gain or is already in possession of nuclear weapons. Those who believe that these countries dislike America solely because of our support for Israel, our entrance into Mecca, the war in Iraq, or some other action perceived by them as blasphemous, imperialistic, or just plain arrogant and wrong are badly mistaken. These countries have a proven history of despotism, lack of tolerance, severe restrictions on freedom, violations of human rights, and support of terrorism. They tell us every day that they seek our destruction and that of our allies. For example, in certain Iranian mosques, there are chants of "Death to America" every Friday. Certainly, not all Muslims and, I hope, not a majority, but at least a significant number of Muslim leaders, hold the belief that nonbelievers of their religion must be converted to Islam, turned into slaves, or slain. It would seem that these beliefs alone would preclude any compromise or successful negotiations. If the majority of Muslims are moderate, tolerant of others' beliefs, and peaceful (as many believe), it might be helpful if more of this group stood up to be counted and loudly renounced all forms of terrorism, including or perhaps especially, Islamic terrorism.

Concentrated power has always been the enemy of liberty.

—Ronald Reagan

The wants of these rogue nations are unreasonable, unending, and impossible to meet. Compromise, even if we were willing, is not an option for them. They appear to be engaging with us solely as a ploy for more time to develop better weapons. Therefore, they love the idea of "talks" that they view as meaningless but that we perceive as honest negotiations. How many lies regarding critical issues from Iran should it take until we completely distrust them? How many failed attempts to attract many of our feckless allies should it take before we realize that their own domestic agendas preclude them from participating in meaningful sanctions or actions?

Like all tyrannies, Iran and North Korea are interested only in increasing their hold on authority, and their only respect is for power. So power (not time-consuming talk or respectful rhetoric) is what the United States needs to show them. They must understand that there can be devastating consequences to the hateful actions they are contemplating. This is not the time to reduce our military capabilities and no time to rely solely on public relations to protect our country. Why would a Liberal—or anyone else, for that matter—not want a strong defense? Why would anyone in America support a "soft on defense" or "carry no stick" defense strategy?

An appeaser is one who feeds a crocodile,
hoping it will eat him last.

—Winston Churchill

Liberals offer many creative arguments that sound good but once studied, often appear to be based in populist slogans, myth, or an unrealistic worldview. Many Liberals, particularly those who are pacifists, believe in unilateral nuclear disarmament. They seem to think that if we just get rid of all our nuclear weapons, everyone else will follow suit. They are suggesting we carry no stick at all. Conservatives have no appetite to appease those who wish to harm us.

Conservatives believe unequivocally that there is evil in the world and that these rogue nations hate America in large part because we call them what they are and bring attention to their wrongdoing. Many Liberals believe differently. They have the sense that these dictators and tyrants do not hate us because of who we are and what we stand for, but that they are just reacting to what they perceive to be bad American policies. Many Liberals also believe that the otherwise friendly nations who do not join us wholeheartedly in our efforts to combat terrorist nations are doing so not because of their own internal political or economic concerns, but because the United States has not asked them nicely enough or has not displayed adequate humility.

Liberals appease and present new, much more tolerant rhetoric apparently because they believe it was the faulty rhetoric and policies of past Conservative administrations that caused rogue nations to dislike us and caused many of our allies to not join us. In other words, many Liberals blame America (or at least Conservatives in America) for the lack of cordial and cooperative relations with these countries. Personally, once these rogue nations start stoning their women for getting raped, imprisoning or killing their citizens for expressing their own views, or cutting off people's heads just to make a point, I no longer believe that changing U.S. policies or talking nicely will do much to impress them. As to our allies, many will need to see direct evidence of the threats to their countries or actual terrorist attacks on their soil before they join our effort to defeat terrorists.

Patriots versus Terrorists
Start Game: Choose Weapons

Who would not be for strong defense?

Liberals appear to make up the majority of the "blame America first" crowd and seem to not see America as a fundamentally good and caring country with sound moral values. Apparently, these people cannot see the millions of people around the world who have been liberated by American blood and treasury. But they do seem to be able to seize on the mistakes of a few Americans and use these individuals' atypical actions to condemn the whole. There are too many people in our country who can rattle off every mistake they perceive Americans have ever made but just cannot recall very much of the good.

The Progressive mentality often reflects moral equivalence. *Moral equivalence* is a term used in political debate that can be defined as treating two or more moral behaviors representing different degrees of wrongdoing without distinction. An exaggerated example might be when a serious wrongdoing, such as ethnic cleansing, is presented as similar to a much lesser wrongdoing, such as stealing or mugging. For these people, America, because of its war efforts against terrorist nations, can be presented as just as evil as a totalitarian nation that supports terrorist acts on innocent people. This type of argument often occurs when one side believes itself to be morally superior to the other. Therefore, because of their perceived moral superiority, they can rationalize equating a serious offense to society with a minor one.

For example, you have likely heard the claim by some that the terrorist events of 9/11 happened because we in the United States brought it on ourselves with our antiterrorist policies or our support for Israel. The grossly illogical assumption here is that the 9/11 terrorists were somehow justified in killing more than three thousand innocent Americans and foreign nationals. Fortunately, this is a perception offered by only the extreme radical Left, and it is not a view held by mainstream Liberals or Conservatives.

The fallacy of this thinking lies in the implied argument of moral equivalency (i.e., some U.S. soldiers wrongfully humiliated POWs in Abu Ghraib prison; therefore, the United States lacks the moral authority to denounce human rights violations around the world). The fatal flaw is this type of argument represents a completely illogical comparison between two offenses very different in seriousness or degree of immorality. Although both acts were wrong, there is just no moral equivalence between humiliating a POW and al-Qaeda's horrendous act of beheading an American news reporter. The embarrassments that occurred in the Abu Ghraib prison are of a college-hazing magnitude and just cannot be equated with murder and mutilation. In addition, when the U.S. military discovered the behavior at Abu Ghraib, it adjudicated, disciplined, and imprisoned the perpetrators. On the other hand, the al-Qaeda operatives who killed the innocent American videotaped the brutal exercise and advertised their pride in committing such an act.

Conservatives believe there is a clear line between right and wrong and that some wrongs represent much worse offenses than others. Conservatives see radical terrorists who hide behind their own version of Islam as evil people, and Conservatives make this judgment with no equivocations and with no hint of the moral equivalence seen by some others.

If the battle for civilization comes down to the wimps versus the barbarians, the barbarians are going to win.

—Thomas Sowell

A prisoner of war is a man who tries to kill you and fails, and then asks you not to kill him.

—Winston Churchill

Furthermore, many Liberals seem to have very selective outrage; they chose Bosnia over Rwanda and the genocide in Darfur over that in Iraq. Plus, once the Iraq war became unpopular, Liberals "forgot" about their vote to authorize force in Iraq and irrationally painted the war in Afghanistan as the good one and the war in Iraq as the bad one. We are now bogged down in Afghanistan, a tribal place where no one—including Genghis Kahn, the British, and the Russians—has ever been able to establish an enduring peace or a stable government. My concern is not that America does not have the might to win this war in Afghanistan; my concern is that if this war becomes unpopular (as it did in Iraq), many in America could lose the political will to win.

If you are not prepared to use force to defend civilization,
then be prepared to accept barbarism.

—Thomas Sowell

Once the war in Iraq became a political liability to Liberals, they began to call for a timetable for leaving or quitting the war. They were willing to accept defeat, and in fact, many leading Liberals actually claimed that defeat had already occurred. To many, this seemed completely un-American.

Like a baseball game, wars are not over till they are over.
Wars don't run on a clock like football. No previous generation was
so hopelessly unrealistic that this had to be explained to them.

—Thomas Sowell

No one has said America is perfect, but the fact that America's compassion and kindness have enabled so many people around the world to enjoy so much freedom is a good and noble stance. This is why America is revered by other peace-loving countries and why multitudes of people from other nations desire to come to America and eventually become American citizens. How many people are attempting to sneak into Iran or North Korea? How many foreign nationals want to become citizens of these countries?

The founding fathers and Conservatives would argue that the federal entitlement programs rarely "promote enduring general welfare," but there is no doubt a strong defense and a "peace through strength" strategy plays an important role in the government's ability to protect its people and to "provide for the common defense."

In addition to protecting our country from foreign enemies, our government's near-equal responsibility is to protect our society from itself and to ensure our safety from domestic harm (i.e., criminals).

Principle 2: Ensure Domestic Tranquility

Principle 2: Ensure Domestic Tranquility, Efficient and Effective Law Enforcement, and a Fair and Impartial Justice System

To make the criminal justice system work properly, federal, state, and local law-enforcement agencies (including the judicial system) need the professional capacity to catch and detain criminal suspects, provide them with a fair and just trial, make the punishments fit the crime, and carry out the judicial sentences. These are important and obvious fundamentals in promoting and ensuring domestic tranquility.

A key element in domestic protections is what many Conservatives refer to as "tough on crime." That does not imply unduly harsh penalties for anyone convicted of any crime; it indicates only that the law enforcement and judicial system mete out punishments consistent with the offenses committed. In other words, those who commit minor crimes are treated accordingly; those who commit major crimes may receive as much as life imprisonment or the death penalty.

Domestic tranquility is assured when our government provides a fair and impartial judiciary (federal, state, and local courts) combined with fair and impartial domestic law enforcement, which includes the FBI, state highway patrol, county sheriffs, and local police. The point

Tough on Crime: Who would be for soft on crime?

here is that for the jurisprudence system to work, everyone in it, including the perpetrators of crime, need to know that the sentence will fit the crime: the greater or lesser the consequences of the crime or the offense to society, the greater or lesser the punishment.

Our laws represent each individual's responsibility to his fellow man. Not only do the punishments of those convicted of breaking our laws need to deter other criminals, but they also need to make a strong impact on the noncriminal society's, or the public's, mind. In other words, the sentence given to convicted criminals needs to not only condemn the offense to society, but also send a strong message to all in society that there will be proportionate punishments, not just rhetorical condemnations, of illegal and irresponsible behavior. Everyone in our country needs to understand that our society will not tolerate bad behavior, especially when it interferes with the rights and liberties of others. Thus, in spite of its many imperfections (including the many judicial and jury misjudgments, and occasional prosecutorial zealotry), our country's fair and impartial criminal law enforcement has been not only a critical element in the protection of society, but also an important contributor to our country's success as a free nation.

Conservatives believe it is not the role of judges or justices (sometimes called "activist judges") to use the courtroom as a vehicle to "write" new law by reinterpreting the Constitution or other laws to fit the judge's ideology or his or her personal notion of fairness. That is, the role of a judge or justice is to hear the facts and to interpret the law and the Constitution as it was originally written and intended. It is not their right to use their decisions and judgments in the courtroom to "correct" what they might perceive as social wrongs in society or to mete out their sentences based on their personal or political beliefs.

Furthermore, Conservatives understand that the laws passed at the federal and state levels must not conflict with the rights and limitations stated in the Constitution. And as long as these state and federal laws are constitutional, they also must be interpreted as written and intended. In essence, Conservatives believe the Constitution, as it was written, is the final authority when it comes to matters of law. If one wants to change it, there is a process called constitutional amendment, in which both Congress and the citizens have the opportunity to vote on any proposed revisions to the Constitution.

Who believes being tough on crime is wrong? Who would argue for being soft on crime?

There are those in our society who lean toward treating criminals as victims of society. It is their belief that most, if not all, convicted criminals are basically good people who require only rehabilitation and reeducation to turn them off their path of crime and violence. They often express the notion that if jails and penitentiaries offered more amenities and made inmates more comfortable during their prison stays, society would be rewarded with influxes of reinstated citizens who would abide by the laws and become productive members of the community for perhaps the first time in their misbegotten lives. People who believe in this philosophy often describe themselves as Liberals or Progressives.

Progressives often push for "treatment," not detainment and punishment, and make arguments to make life easier for criminals. Conservatives tend to support the sentencing of convicted criminals to hard work and much more austere but humane living conditions. The progressive worldview holds that the criminal is not entirely responsible for his crime, but that the crime was, at least in part, the fault of imperfections or flaws in society. So when a criminal is convicted, it is often the Progressive position that the prisoner should be rehabilitated and given additional rights and benefits. It is their sense, in spite of fifty years of contrary evidence, that criminals will come out of jail as better people if the jails are more pleasant and that the criminals will come out worse if the jails are harsher. It has been clearly shown that what occurs in "easy" jails is not a greater level of rehabilitation, but a much greater level of recidivism.

Liberals, Progressives, and their activist judges appear to believe that it is government's role to correct social injustice. For example, they often feel that if an individual is a pedophile, thief, or rapist, that person likely was a victim of some social or economic injustice. Therefore, they see it as the government's role to correct or to compensate for what they perceive as pervasive social ills. Liberals have a tendency to think in terms of moral relativism; that is, nothing is really bad, and there is always a valid rationale or reason that explains the transgression. A Conservative will usually see a bright line between right and wrong. With very few exceptions, they see pedophiles, thieves, and rapists as being personally responsible for having done wrong. Progressives do not see such a distinct line. Too often, they see hapless victims who likely have been forced to do wrong by circumstances beyond their control.

The Progressive mindset holds on to a notion that tougher jails that require hard labor produce harder and more belligerent criminals, irrespective of all the evidence to the contrary. Many take this illogical position either because they have not reviewed the research and the facts on the subject or because taking this position makes them feel better about themselves and society as a whole. Liberals can often be heard saying that it is better to spend our money on prevention rather than to waste it on jails. Conservatives also believe this to be a noble goal, but just like the proven ineffectiveness of "soft" jails, there is a flaw in this argument. Our society has tried many times to fund prevention programs, but so far they just have not worked. It seems the Liberal positions on this matter (and many others) are often more about feelings and psychic satisfaction than reason.

The Progressive is often satisfied if the programs they are supporting (e.g., soft jails or funding prevention) sound noble and well intentioned, in spite of the efficacy of those programs. The Conservative is all for testing the waters with programs designed to achieve noble goals but is also willing to abandon or modify these programs if the tests fail. The Liberal tendency is often to just throw more money at a failing program while blaming the failure on an uncaring or unenlightened society. Conservatives are more likely to pursue a different and more proven course of action while they continue to search for better and more effective ways to help society.

Therefore, Conservatives are tough on crime not because they are mean, unenlightened, or uncaring, but because they are committed to protecting society with proven policies and programs; and they are not satisfied with just being able to say "we tried" or "we had good intentions" or "everyone agrees our goals are noble."

Principle 3: The Right to Self-defense

Principle 3: The Right to Self-defense (including the Second Amendment, often referred to as the Right to Bear Arms)

If the first two institutional levels of protection are not entirely successful, Conservatives believe in the third level, which is the right to self-defense. The government's first responsibility is to protect its citizens from harm. A strong defense protects us militarily from harm from foreign enemies, and our government is also committed to protect us from internal criminal harm. The forces of a strong military, a fair and just jurisprudence system, superior domestic law enforcement, and constitutionally guaranteed individual liberties and limits on government authority are all designed to work in concert to promote individual opportunity and domestic tranquility. However, our founders recognized that institutional protections alone might not be enough and bestowed on all of us the absolute right to protect ourselves.

Americans have the right and advantage of being armed— unlike the citizens of other countries whose governments are afraid to trust the people with arms.

—James Madison

According to the second amendment, the government does not have the right to prevent its citizens from owning guns.

The second amendment reads:

"A well regulated Militia, being necessary to the security of a free State, the right of the people to keep and bear Arms, shall not be infringed."

Throughout history, leftist and dictatorial governments such as the National Socialist Party (Nazis), who won without a majority, could not have remained in existence with an armed citizenry. One of their early steps to protect their power was to confiscate civilian arms, largely enabling them to institute their draconian policies. There has been much discussion about the founders' reasoning behind the Second Amendment. However, irrespective of all of their reasoning (e.g., to allow citizens to help in case of enemy attack, to protect the citizenry from a too-strong central government, or for self-defense against a potential criminal force), their intent seems altogether clear. Our founders intended for us to be able to arm ourselves with more than just rocks, fists, and harsh words.

With the Right to Own Guns, We the People Are Citizens;
Without the Right to Own Guns, We the People Are Subjects

> *The beauty of the Second Amendment is that*
> *it will not be needed until they try to take it.*
>
> —Thomas Jefferson

Who would be opposed to "the right to self-defense"?

Through Liberal reinterpretation of the Constitution, many liberals have shown that they disagree with this sense of the Second Amendment.

Progressives always seem to be working for more and more gun control. Obviously they blame the guns, not the criminals, for gun-related crimes. This logic would cause us to blame pencils for misspelled words or rocks for broken windows. Liberals seem unconcerned that excessive gun control will likely leave only the criminals with guns. Also, Liberals appear to see many elements of self-defense such as the right to bear arms and to personally defend self, family, and property as an offense to civilized society. Many Liberals speak as though they believe the whole notion of self-defense and owning guns is barbaric. Further, Liberals believe citizens' having guns provokes more violent attacks. The Progressive agenda against individual gun ownership would have us unilaterally disarm ourselves, knowing that this action would make us easier prey and more tempting targets for well-armed criminals, as it has in Great Britain. It is difficult to see how making the citizenry of our country more vulnerable would make us a safer society.

The three levels of protection are necessary and of the highest priority of government. Conservatives believe the only thing tyrants and despots respect is the perception of power. Therefore, Conservatives opt for the "carry a very big stick" approach. As history has verified, when tyrants see weakness, they will attack;

when criminals are shown more compassion, they will commit more crimes. That is, when consequences or punishments are not commensurate with the evil deeds they've perpetrated, criminals have no reason not to repeat their crimes.

The Progressive agenda of being "soft on foreign policy," "soft on crime," and "soft on criminals" is just too dangerous. Many Liberals seem to believe in "Speak softly and carry no stick, ignore tyrannical repression, and continually apologize for perceived past American mistakes." Unilateral disarmament is beyond foolish, and anyone who would take steps to make our national defense weaker has buried his or her head in the sand.

Humble rhetoric alone will not deter international bullies, and criminals will not be reformed by just giving them TVs, workout rooms, Internet access, conjugal visits, and libraries. I believe criminals will get the picture when they know the punishments will be as severe as their crimes; they will be deterred when they realize that if they attack someone's home, there is the potential they could be shot dead.

Parable #2

"Take a Stand for the Stand!"

As the long, hot, summer days dragged on, the lemonade stand got more and more business. Everybody stopped by for lemonade—kids, moms, dads, grandparents, and even the volunteer firefighters. Some days, Tommy and his friends could hardly keep up with all the business. They had to add on to the stand to handle the customers. Robbie's little brother helped out now and then.

They were making some serious money that summer.

But the boys knew one thing. They had to keep their customers happy.

"Sometimes," said Tommy, "when you're drinking a cup of lemonade, you want something to eat too. Maybe we oughta be sellin' some food too. What do you think?"

Well, John, Benny, Robbie, and Roger thought it was a pretty awesome idea. So they started selling chocolate chip cookies that Benny's mom made—little kids loved those—and they had muffins for the grown-ups. Their lemonade stand just got more and more popular.

Things couldn't have been better. But then, toward the end of June, a new family moved in on the block. The Benedicts had two girls, twins, and a boy they called Little Arnie. They were a nice family, a friendly group, and the girls even helped out at the stand sometimes. But Little Arnie . . . whoa, he was something else.

He was the fastest talker you ever heard, and he never, ever stopped talking, not even to breathe. "Hi, guess what, my name's Arnie and I'm new here, guess what, we live in that really, really big house, and guess what, my dad's really, really good friends with the mayor, and guess what, I know some really, really big movie stars." Chances were he talked like that in his sleep.

John, Benny, Roger, and Robbie thought the new kid was just sort of . . . different. But Tommy had a feeling that Little Arnie wasn't what he seemed.

It was true Arnie was more than a talker. He was a kid with big ideas. From the first minute he saw the lemonade stand, Little Arnie wanted to be part of it. He had all kinds of plans and schemes, and he wasn't shy about sharing them. "Guess what, I know how ya can make a ton more money, really, really easy, guess what it is, OK, I'll tell ya, all ya do is put in one less lemon and use more water, and guess what, nobody'll know the difference!"

"We'll know the difference," Tommy told him.

But the others weren't so sure. "Maybe Arnie's right," they told Tommy. "Wouldn't hurt to try it."

And they did try it. On the next batch of lemonade, they used one less lemon.

And nobody seemed to notice.

After that, Little Arnie started sharing more and more of his ideas. "OK, guess what, now we're gonna cut out two lemons." . . . "Why do ya put so many chips in these chocolate chip cookies, huh?" . . . "I have an idea, guess what it is, I'll tell ya, we oughta be charging extra for cups!" . . . "Ya wanna know what we need, I'll tell ya, what we need is a lemonade stand on every corner in the city!"

Some of the guys were jazzed about Arnie's big ideas, but not Tommy. He called John, Benny, Roger, and Robbie over to his house that night. "We have a hard enough time with one lemonade stand," Tommy told his friends. "If we try to run more, they won't be as good. We're just not ready yet."

Tommy was right and the others knew it. It took everything they had to keep the stand running. "And there's one more thing," he said. "Our lemonade doesn't taste as good since we cut back on lemons. You know it and I know it."

And he was right about that too. They decided to make it the way they had before Little Arnie came along.

The next day was another hot day and the kids sold about a million gallons of lemonade. Little Arnie didn't show up until after lunch. "Guess what, I got a really, really great idea for ya, guess what it is, I'll tell ya, it's a lemonade stand on wheels, what do ya think, huh, is that a really, really great idea or what?" Then he said, "Seems I've been having *all* the ideas lately, doesn't it? Seems you oughta let me run the stand now, what do you think?"

But Tommy said, "No, Arnie." And the others stood behind him on this. "You're not gonna take our lemonade stand." And they told him that they were dropping all his ideas—no more cutting back on lemons, no scrimping on chocolate chips, or charging for cups.

Arnie didn't say anything for a minute. Then he said, "My dad knows the mayor."

And Tommy said, "You're not gonna take our lemonade stand."

Arnie said, "I . . . I have friends. Big, mean friends. I might just give 'em a call."

And they all said, "You're not gonna take our lemonade stand."

The boys weren't sure what Little Arnie was going to do next. But here's what happened.

He started to cry. Little Arnie started to cry like a baby. He had a full-scale, all-out tantrum right there on the sidewalk. He ran home and the kids hardly saw him for the rest of that long, hot summer.

The moral of the story: A strong defense is necessary to preserve our individual rights.

Note to parents: This story is an analogy of our country's strategy of peace through strength. The lemonade stand, like our country, is able to operate because Tommy anticipated a problem and he was prepared to defend the stand.

Chapter 9

The Economic System of Conservatism

Principle 4: Capitalism
Principle 5: Property Rights
Principle 6: Free Trade
Principle 7: Fiscal Responsibility

The Declaration of Independence holds that certain truths (i.e., "all men are created equal") are self-evident and that all men "are endowed by their Creator with certain unalienable rights, that among these are life, liberty, and the pursuit of happiness." The first three Conservative principles of strong defense, domestic tranquility, and the right to self-defense were largely focused on the right to "life." These three principles were selected first to reflect a sense of priorities as the concept relates to citizen concerns and government responsibilities. It appears that our founding fathers might have also believed that securing the country, assuring an atmosphere of domestic tranquility, and providing for the right to self-defense were foundational issues that, if met, would set the stage for additional rights of the people to live in liberty and to seek happiness and prosperity.

Our country's founders supported these next four principles of Conservatism in order to move the country further toward completion of the founders' original equation (which includes life, liberty, and the pursuit of happiness). It was the founders' general intention that the government provide a safe and secure environment while ensuring each individual's right to pursue happiness in whatever way each citizen felt best, as long as his or her choices did not infringe on another citizen's right to do the same. In other words, the founders knew that some form of government was needed to do that which could not be effectively carried out by individuals or individual states, but they were concerned that a too-strong central government could lead them back into the oppression they had just fought to overcome.

Our founders also understood the need to offer an economic opportunity for individual prosperity consistent with the moral sensibilities of the people of our new nation and the general welfare of the nation's greater society. The structure and foundation of this opportunity turned out to be what we now call Free-Market Capitalism. Our founders supported Free-Market Capitalism by establishing a limited government that allowed for an atmosphere of individual freedom for all citizens to pursue their self-interests that was free from arbitrary and unnecessary government rules, regulations, and taxes.

Adam Smith's style of Capitalism provided each citizen of our new nation the opportunity to improve his station in life without having to rely on government handouts or resorting to less-than-moral means. Free-Market Capitalism has provided a moral economic framework that has given America and individual Americans the greatest peace and prosperity that has ever been known to man. Through the private ownership of business and enterprise, Capitalism provided an equal opportunity for each and every American to become successful based not on their station in life or birthright, but on their own efforts.

Free-Market Capitalism is not only a key element of Conservatism; it is also the engine that creates both individual and societal prosperity, which in turn supports the infrastructure needed to keep America safe. The Conservative principles of property rights, free trade, and fiscal responsibility discussed later in this chapter support the economic system of Capitalism.

Principle 4: Capitalism

Conservatives believe in Capitalism, and as long as business and enterprise is operated within the law, Conservatives also believe the following to be true and moral:

- It is OK to make money.
- It is OK for a company to make a profit.
- It is OK for companies and individuals to be successful.
- It is even OK for a person to be rich.

These outcomes are not necessarily good things in and of themselves, but neither are they bad things, and they are not inconsistent with American sensibilities or moral behavior!

Some people regard private enterprise as a predatory tiger to be shot. Others look on it as a cow they can milk. Not enough people see it as a healthy horse, pulling a sturdy wagon.

—Winston Churchill

Definition of Capitalism

What is Capitalism? It is an economic system that allows and promotes privately owned, wealth-producing enterprises.

Each person owns his own individual labor and can use it as he decides within the boundaries of his own needs, the rules of law, and a limited framework of regulations. Capitalism is built around the concept that an enterprise has the opportunity to be successful as dictated by market-driven economics (as opposed to government-central, planning-driven economics). Capitalism is a system wherein individuals have the opportunity to be personally rewarded for their individual achievements by following their natural instincts and tendencies to pursue self-interest in a morality-based economic system that provides an equal opportunity for all to achieve success. It has the added advantage of its capacity to improve the circumstances of society and community. Everyone has equal opportunity to achieve, no matter his background, age, or race.

Like a Rising Tide Raises All Ships

Without Free-Market Capitlalism, the next best alternative is Socialism, Fascism, or Communism.

Capitalism knows only one color: that color is green;
all else is necessarily subservient to it, hence, race, gender,
and ethnicity cannot be considered within it.

—Unknown Author

What Is the Origin of Capitalism in America?

When the Pilgrims first came to America, many were eager for religious freedom. The settlers knew that to ensure their freedom of religion, they needed to establish some new form of authority, but they were not entirely sure about the kind of authority they wanted or needed. They were wary of a too-strong central government such as they experienced first under King Charles I and eventually under King George III in Great Britain, but they also knew that having no formal local or central authority (anarchy) would produce only chaos. Over the next hundred years and under the distant thumb of Great Britain and others, they tried many forms of governance, but each was lacking in one respect or another.

One of the forms of government they attempted was a form of Socialism, in which a neighborhood or community was operated somewhat like a commune. The governance system was designed for each member of the community to provide for the entire community by adding what he produced to a stock for everyone to use. This style of government did not succeed because the settlers found that some participants did not produce or provide their fair share. Eventually the form of government that worked best was when the people were able to keep what they produced, first taking care of themselves and their families then taking their extra produce to the market to trade or sell to acquire other goods and services they could not produce on their own. Although various elements of

Capitalism had been tried for centuries in other parts of the world, this was the beginning of American Free-Market Capitalism.

The Origins and Foundations of Capitalism

In his 1776 book *The Wealth of Nations*, Adam Smith provided what is often considered the seminal work on modern economics. Smith offered that a key element in the success of Capitalism was that its process was consistent with an element of human nature that he described as ruthless individualism. He explained how self-interest, based in moral reason and a free-market economy, could lead to economic well-being for both the productive individual as well as all of society. Liberals often refer to this natural self-interest as "greed" to rationalize their desire for more government intervention into the everyday lives of people. Also, Liberals are generally reticent to keep score, many believing this unnecessarily harms the psyches of the losers. However, Conservatives believe that most people are naturally competitive, like to keep score, and feel a responsibility to take care of their own families and communities.

Why Free-Market Capitalism Works

Free enterprise is the ability to buy, sell, and trade goods and services with minimal or no government interference.

---

*It is not from the benevolence of the butcher,
the brewer, or the baker, that we can expect our dinner,
but from their regard to their own interest.*

—Adam Smith

Charity, when money is given rather than earned, while a virtuous act, cannot alone provide the essentials for living. Self-interest is the mechanism that can remedy the shortcoming.

That is, any business in America, from an individual baker to an enterprise such as today's Apple Corporation, engages in the work it does first and foremost to satisfy its self-interest. In other words, they all do what they do in order to achieve success and security for themselves and their families. However, although their primary motivation (or in some cases only motivation) might be to improve their personal circumstances in life, the process of producing a needed service or an improved product benefits all in society. In addition, the "invisible hand" of Adam Smith's marketplace determines a fair value for the commodities they are selling and those they are buying. In the free market, an exchange takes place only when both parties benefit.

Thus, in *The Wealth of Nations*, Smith established the economic doctrine of free enterprise, "the invisible hand" of the marketplace, and "how self-interest guides the most efficient use of resources in a nation's economy . . . while public welfare comes as a by-product." It was Adam Smith's belief that the "invisible hand" of markets with now millions of people making buying- and selling-related decisions to determine prices and values was infinitely more fair and accurate than the often arbitrary or politically motivated prices and values set by the central planners of government.

Benefits of Capitalism

Capitalism is designed to reward achievement. Those whose skills and talents are honed and are in demand have the opportunity to be highly rewarded, and in some cases, very highly rewarded. The fact that some individuals and some companies have exploited business opportunities and have been hugely compensated is a superb example of American ingenuity. Being innovative and making a lot of money from that innovation *is* the American dream.

This is the case even though some have been and will continue to be rewarded for just being in the right place at the right time, and some will even be rewarded for being born into the right circumstances. The "invisible hand" of the marketplace is not perfect, but it is highly superior to whatever is in second place. This is a good example of not letting "perfect" be the enemy of "good." Rewarding achievers is good! Rewarding successful innovators, risk-takers, and entrepreneurs is good. Not all innovation and business success will stand the test of time. Some products and services will be in demand today and forgotten tomorrow. However, it is still best to let an impartial market made up of millions of individual citizens, including millions of individual producers, sellers, and customers, decide the winners and losers.

Of course, Free-Market Capitalism does not ensure absolute fairness. Not everyone agrees with the value placed on some items in the marketplace. Most people would not agree with the marketplace determination that movie actors or other entertainers receive higher compensation than do teachers, police, or firefighters. These kinds of wage inequities could encourage government regulation or turn one away from Free-Market Capitalism. However, on the whole the marketplace does a fairly good job of determining value based on supply and demand, and the next best alternative to Free-Market Capitalism is completely unacceptable. Communism, Fascism, Socialism, and many other forms of government have all been sold to large numbers of people based on the argument that their approach to governance is the most fair and compassionate way to run a country. History has clearly shown that these other forms of government are not only unfair, but also oppressive and often unable to sustain even themselves.

*Entrepreneurs and their small enterprises are responsible
for almost all the economic growth in the United States.*

—Ronald Reagan

Why Progressives Generally Dislike Capitalism

The Liberal approach to governance all too often serves to *punish the successful;* they regularly attribute negative traits to those who receive higher compensation and ignore the virtues of sacrifice and hard work of the majority of these high earners. It appears that in many Liberal minds, the highly compensated are guilty (of something) unless proven innocent. The implication is that the highly compensated must have done something unethical or wrong to achieve their success. It is easy to see, however, what appears to be selective outrage. For many Liberals, there seem to be certain exceptions in their condemnations of the well paid (e.g., Hollywood entertainers, musicians, athletes, those who make their money from "green" businesses, trust-fund babies, civil litigation attorneys, union leaders, and Liberal politicians). Many Liberal elites severely criticize private company perks, which they view as excessive and insensitive, but are perfectly comfortable with such items as private jets and expensive junkets for Congress. Could it be that certain Progressives believe in egalitarianism for the masses but not for the elites? I will leave it to you to make your own judgments as to the reasons for these apparent exceptions.

The Progressive philosophy regularly equates disparate outcomes with illegal or unethical discrimination. They feel there must have been some level of victimhood for those on the losing side of this equation because of societal bias or some unfair advantage of those on the winning side of this equation. In other words, when one individual makes more than another, the Liberal tendency is often to see the individual who makes less as a victim and the individual who makes more as having done something wrong. With this kind of thinking, it is easy to see why Liberals might be suspicious of Capitalism and skeptical of its potential benefits. It is also easy to see why many Liberals believe that government, not the free market, should "correct" what they see as inequities.

The inherent vice of Capitalism is the unequal sharing of blessings; the inherent virtue of Socialism is the equal sharing of miseries.

—Winston Churchill

If an elected official (or someone running for elected office) can convince his constituency that the system consists primarily of victims and cheaters, then the elected official can introduce programs to support or compensate the "victims" and to punish or unreasonably tax the "cheaters." Most of the people who benefit from Capitalism have worked hard to exploit whatever opportunities they have found. There are, of course, real-life cheaters and real-life victims. The cheaters need to be dealt with swiftly and fairly, and the victims need to be helped by society. In general, however, the opportunities of Capitalism are moral and fair, and those who have achieved success have earned it.

Looking at a real-life example, how many people would give up a long and hard twelve to fourteen years of life to become educated and skilled in the medical profession if the financial incentives to do so were drastically reduced? The answer seems obvious. Who would benefit if there were fewer doctors? Again, the answer seems obvious. Free-Market Capitalism places a societal value on doctors that up until now has generated a substantial number of medical professionals. Like nearly everyone else, doctors want to do good, but they also want to do well for themselves and their families. Conservatives believe that although the marketplace is not perfect in determining relative value, it is far superior to big-government central planning. Pundits often express their view that those in the medical profession ought to perform their duties for little or no profit. These same people, however, believe that the marketplace should be the determining factor of their own compensation. This seems, at the very least, to be a bit hypocritical and, at the worst, to be ignorant of human nature.

Everyone in society would lose if our nation produced fewer doctors. No one would gain if our country lost its best and brightest doctors to nonmedical endeavors. The thinking that would artificially reduce the compensation of doctors (by government decree) is an example of a fairly noble Liberal idea to reduce the cost of health care for everyone with the likely unintended consequence of deteriorating the quality and quantity of health care for everyone. This seems like another example of Progressive programs that have objectives that sound good but just do not work. Perhaps if Liberals believe that doctors are charging too much, they should spend the twelve to fourteen years and $150,000 to $250,000 to become a doctor then charge less for their services.

I was recently asked why teachers are not more highly paid (relative to doctors) since their compensation is set by the government and without teachers, there would be no doctors. The answer lies partially in an imperfect marketplace. Plus, doctors generally must dedicate more time to become qualified to practice medicine than teachers do to teach. There is, however, another material factor. Teachers work in a unionized environment that does not measure or reward individual success. In other words, a teacher with exceptional skills cannot be paid more for consistently delivering extraordinary student achievement. By contract, most teachers can only increase their compensation through greater seniority or obtaining more degrees. These union contracts do provide benefits to teachers, and they are particularly effective at protecting weak teachers. However, this "protection," which strives to make sure that all teachers are treated equally, comes at a significant cost. Unlike many free-market industries, excellence in teaching cannot be rewarded under the existing system.

In general, why do Liberals place big-government central planning ahead of Free-Market Capitalism? This question is especially difficult to answer when the history of central planning (think the Soviet Union and many developing nations) have failed so miserably. Those Progressives who consider themselves to be part of the intellectual elite might actually believe that although their numbers are few, they can determine outcomes and values more accurately than the "invisible hand" of the free market, consisting of millions of people making billions of decisions.

The Liberal rationale for government central planning over Free-Market Capitalism appears to be based on many false assumptions:

- Individuals might not be smart or educated enough to make the "right" decisions for themselves.
- The rich have made their money off the backs of poor people.
- The economic pie is static, which results in a zero-sum game where in order for someone to become wealthy, someone else must become poor.
- There is no virtuous way to become successful.
- "Fairness" and "social justice" demand that the government redistribute wealth to correct societal disadvantages.

- Disparate outcomes must be due to disparate opportunities or unfair advantages to those who succeed.
- Government officials are generally altruistic and immune to self-interest.
- Self-interest is an immoral vice of human nature, which must be corrected.
- The structure of government can be both efficient and effective.
- The majority of nonachievers are victims of society.
- Greed and corruption exist primarily in private enterprise and are less prevalent in government organizations.
- Government can give to someone without taking from someone else.
- High taxes on some things, such as cigarettes or gasoline, will reduce their use, but high taxes on entrepreneurship or capital will have no perceivable impact.

In answering Liberal accusations and allegations about the greed and vice of Capitalism, it might be helpful to review the words of economist Milton Friedman, who in this passage was answering a Liberal TV interviewer who was prodding him on the evils of Capitalism. The interviewer asked, "*When you see around the globe the maldistribution of wealth, the desperate plight of millions of people in underdeveloped countries, when you see so few haves and so many have-nots, when you see the greed and the concentration of power, did you ever have a moment of doubt about Capitalism and whether greed is a good idea to run on?*"

Friedman answered, "*Well, first of all tell me, is there some society you know that doesn't run on greed? You think Russia doesn't run on greed? Do you think China doesn't run on greed? What is greed? Of course, none of us are greedy; it's only the other fella that's greedy. The world runs on individuals pursuing their separate interests. The greatest achievements of civilization have not come from government bureaus. Einstein didn't construct his theory under order from a bureaucrat. Henry Ford didn't revolutionize the automobile industry that way. In the only cases in which the masses have escaped from the kind of grinding poverty you're talking about, the only cases in recorded history are where they have had Capitalism and largely free trade. If you want to know where the masses are worst off, it's exactly in the kind of societies that depart from that.*

"So that the record of history is absolutely crystal clear, that there is no alternative way, so far discovered, of improving the lot of the ordinary people that can hold a candle to the productive activities that are unleashed by a free-enterprise system."

Another argument against Capitalism is that it is not virtuous and that people in the Capitalist system are manipulative and tricky. The interviewer responded to Friedman with this statement, "*But it seems to reward not virtue as much as the ability to manipulate the system.*"

Friedman answered, "*And what does reward virtue? You think the Communist commissar rewards virtue? You think a Hitler rewards virtue? You think American presidents—excuse me, if you'll pardon me—do you think American presidents reward virtue? Do they choose their appointees on the basis of the virtue of the people appointed or on the basis of their political clout? Is it really true that political self-interest is nobler somehow than economic self-interest? You know, I think you're taking a lot of things for granted. And just tell me where in the world you find these angels who are going to organize society for us? Well, I don't even trust you to do that.*"

Friedman's sentiment shows us that Capitalism is not perfect, but its history has proven the incredible success of taking more people out of poverty and has done the most good for the most people, most of the time.

Profit is good. Profit is not the money you bring home to buy the mansion, profit is the money you need to reinvest into your business to keep it competitive. As Peter Drucker said, "A company's primary responsibility is to serve its customers. Profit is not a primary goal, but rather an essential condition for the company's continued existence." This keeps America strong, healthy, and wealthy.

Wealth is good. Wealth is necessary to produce a strong defense, raise the standard of living for all citizens, and provide the necessary resources to fund a safety net for the truly needy and helpless members of our society. Wealth is created through individual and collective productivity. Productivity requires innovation, management, strategy, capital, and hard work. Bringing innovation to the marketplace successfully requires the risk of capital, time, and labor. Free-Market Capitalism provides the vehicle necessary to incentivize entrepreneurs and other individuals to take the risks associated with innovation and productivity. Free-Market Capitalism requires that sufficient funds and sufficient rewards be left in the hands of the entrepreneurs and risk-takers.

Government needs to provide incentives to risk-takers. There are many valid purposes for government to levy taxes and fees on the private sector (e.g., strong defense, safety net for the needy, and support of the legal system), but taking money out of the private sector to allow politicians to give paybacks to campaign contributors or to initiate programs designed primarily to buy votes to ensure reelection are not among them.

Here are several reasons Free-Market Capitalism works and offers such terrific opportunities to all in our society:

- It allows individuals to pursue their self-interest while providing a greater good for society.

- It provides a self-sustaining engine for employment.

- It unleashes the innovation that lives within every citizen and does not depend on a few "very smart" people in government to pick winners and losers among ideas, products, or services. Continuous innovation is the primary element required for businesses to sustain prosperity.

- It provides a country with an economic system that promotes public interest by all without relying solely on the altruism of its individual citizenry.

- It promotes cooperation of the citizenry and division of labor on a voluntary basis, and division of labor is an important key to human productivity.

- It allows our economy to be largely self-regulated with a minimum of government intervention. Self-interest gives incentive to the individual to develop and/or provide needed innovative products and services while competition among individuals and individual enterprises holds down the cost.

- It provides a moral way for an individual to better his circumstances in life.

- It recognizes and minimizes the inherent inefficiency and incompetence of government-run organizations.

- It provides a means for keeping our country financially strong and competitive. This strength is required to keep us safe and prosperous. In the long run, the world really is based on survival of the fittest, and Free-Market Capitalism provides the means for our country to remain the fittest.

- It provides incentive for individuals to put in the time and effort to learn and develop sophisticated skills.

- It provides incentive for individuals to voluntarily take on the more dangerous, dirty, or less pleasant tasks of society.

- It provides a means for individuals to remain free to pursue their own chosen interests, our constitutional right to the blessings of liberty and the individual freedoms accorded by the Declaration of Independence.

- It encourages an entire nation to strive for continual increases in productivity, which generates increased safety and prosperity.

- It promotes rewards and compensation based on performance versus those based on class, race, family, connections, religion, special interests, or friendship.

- It promotes personal pride.

- It promotes prudence and responsibility for both family and government.

- Free markets often bring freedom with them; nations that otherwise might not get along often cooperate for economic reasons.

- Capitalism and rugged individualism are all about taking advantage of the creativity and ingenuity of millions of entrepreneurs and hard work. There is no way central planning can compete.

- It allows common people such as me to write a book and express my personal opinions, and it will be up to the marketplace, not government central planners, whether it succeeds or fails.

Conservatism allows the laws and the marketplace to provide the guideposts to fairness; government elitists are not required. Our Constitution and Capitalist ways offer a moral system that by law gives everyone equal opportunity for life, liberty, and the pursuit of happiness.

Principle 5: Property Rights

Property rights: you own what you have earned and they can't take it away from you. What is yours is yours until you decide otherwise.

The statement above, "they can't take it away from you," reflects the essence of the Conservative view in spite of the fact that it is a bit of an overstatement. Of course, Conservatives support

What is yours is yours. They can't take it from you.

Don't Take My Lemonade Stand

the prudent use of *eminent domain*, which refers to the power of the state to appropriate private property for public use. However, Conservatives (or at least this Conservative) are against the growing use of this power to confiscate private property for any purpose other than that for which these powers were originally intended (e.g., utility lines, railroad facilities and tracks, and major highways). Property rights protect individuals from unreasonable or unnecessary government seizure. It serves no proper purpose for the government to confiscate private property from one private citizen to give it to another private citizen. Apparently the laws pertaining to eminent domain are such that they can be interpreted to allow this trespass. Recently the use of eminent domain powers appear more like political paybacks than appropriation for the public welfare, as was originally intended. If a community or an individual sees a particular parcel of land as an eyesore or blight on his town, there is a nongovernment solution: buy it. Let the marketplace, not some bureaucrat or court, decide on its value.

Property rights are human rights. Within certain legal boundaries, the owner of a resource determines its use. This idea was a revolutionary thought back in the days of the Declaration of Independence. King George III and his designates could and did arbitrarily take private property without explanation or just cause. The Constitution forbids this practice in its explicit enumeration of private property rights.

According to Adam Smith, *the expectation of profit from "improving one's stock of capital" rests on private property rights.* It is a belief central to Capitalism that private property rights encourage the property holders to develop the property, generate wealth, and efficiently allocate resources based on the dictates of the market. The concept of property as a right allows for the production of wealth and the improvement of standards of living.

A property right, by definition, is the exclusive authority to determine how a resource is used, whether government, companies, nonprofit organizations, or individuals own the resource. Conservatives realize that the U.S. Capitalist society is dependent on a strong sense of property rights. Our founding fathers thought so as well and included property rights as one of the fundamental rights in the Constitution.

Property rights are necessary for a civilized society as shown in the following sentiments:

The dichotomy between personal liberties and property rights is a false one. Property does not have rights. People have rights.
—Potter Stewart
American judge and associate justice of the U.S. Supreme Court

Property is surely a right of mankind as real as liberty.
—John Adams, second president of the United States

*Next to the right of liberty, the right of property
is the most important individual right guaranteed by the Constitution
and the one which, united with that of personal liberty, has
contributed more to the growth of civilization than any other
institution established by the human race.*
—William Howard Taft
Twenty-seventh president of the United States

*Property is the fruit of labor;
property is desirable; it is a positive good in the world.*
—Abraham Lincoln
Sixteenth president of the United States

Adam Smith believed government should enforce property rights by laws, contracts, grant patents, and copyrights to encourage inventions and new ideas. Government should provide an atmosphere that induces innovation and promotes business. Capitalism cannot work in a vacuum; it needs the framework and structure of our constitutional rights to succeed. Without the government enforcement of property rights, Capitalism cannot provide the funds necessary to ensure peace or to offer the opportunity of prosperity.

The U.S. Constitution provides explicitly for the protection of private property in the Fifth and Fourteenth Amendments:

Fifth Amendment excerpt:

"*. . . Nor be deprived of life, liberty, or property, without due process of law; nor shall private property be taken for public use, without just compensation.*"

Fourteenth Amendment excerpt:

"*No State shall make or enforce any law which shall abridge the privileges or immunities of citizens of the United States; nor shall any State deprive any person of life, liberty, or property, without due process of law.*"

Famous writer and philosopher Ayn Rand had the following to say about property rights and how man earns his right to his own action:

The right to life is the source of all rights—and the right to property is their only implementation. Without property rights, no other rights are possible. Since man has to sustain his life by his own effort, the man who has no right to the product of his effort has no means to sustain his life. . . . Bear in mind that the right to property is a right to action, like all the others: it is not the right to an object, but to the action and consequences of producing or earning that object. It is not a guarantee that a man will earn any property, but only a guarantee that he will own it if he earns it. It is the right to gain, to keep, to use and to dispose of material values.

> —Ayn Rand, *The Virtue of Selfishness*, p. 94

Rand states, **"You own your own labor, you earn it, you own it. It is your right—your life, your property."**

There can be no liberty unless there is economic liberty.

> —Margaret Thatcher

Why would anyone be against private property rights?

Many Liberals believe in a very broad definition of *eminent domain* and use this broad definition to provide presiding government officials with excessive discretion in its application. They often exercise the powers of eminent domain for the benefit of private developers or commercial interests, using the rationale that anything that increases the value of a given tract of land or that might improve the tax base of the community is a sufficient cause to invoke the powers of eminent domain. This is a radical interpretation and an inappropriate use of the eminent domain laws.

Why would anyone invest in a factory, land, or any means of production if the government could just come in and confiscate it? Why risk the resources of time, energy, and capital? Broad interpretation and use of eminent domain sounds more like Cuba, Russia, and Venezuela, where oil companies and other businesses have been "nationalized"—meaning confiscated by the government, than it does America.

Conservatives believe that strong property rights do not conflict with human rights; they *are* human rights. Progressives often complain that "property rights" regularly trump "human rights," which they feel too often results in people's not being treated "fairly." Of course, what they mean is that certain constituencies of theirs who have not earned and, therefore, do not own substantial property might be at an economic disadvantage to property owners. This is just another argument for redistribution of wealth under the guise of "fairness." Obviously those who have worked for and earned property deserve it. Our founding fathers guaranteed equal opportunity, not equal outcome. Conservatives believe the rights of individuals should determine how resources (e.g., property, land, factory, and means of production) are used with limited interference from the government. Conservatives support the rights of individuals to determine how resources are used with limited interference from government.

Conservatives believe in restricted public use of eminent domain. Property rights ensure that a person owns what he has earned and that what is owned remains owned until one decides to sell it.

Principle 6: Free Trade

Like property rights, free trade is another important value or Conservative principle that is a necessary cog in the engine of Capitalism and American prosperity. Free trade, in its purest form, would allow trading among nations without government interference. In reality, free-trade policies reflect minimal or fewer government interventions into the marketplace such as subsidies, taxes, tariffs, regulatory legislations, or quotas. Free-trade agreements allow for supply and demand to set values in the marketplace, whereas government interventions allow bureaucrats to set these values.

A free market is a healthy market.

The government will still be protecting which jobs from the 1960s?

Conservatives believe that free trade leads to "a race to the top" that expands economic output and increases incomes and standards of living for all. Adam Smith supported the rationality and accuracy of the economic law of comparative advantage. The law of comparative advantage states that it is economically advantageous for each member in a group of trading partners to specialize in and produce the goods in which they possess the lowest opportunity costs relative to the other trading partners. This specialization permits trading partners to then exchange their goods produced as a function of this focus on competitive capabilities. Adam Smith held that this type of specialization maximizes labor, wealth, and quantity of goods produced and, therefore, exceeds what an equal number of independent states could produce in the absence of this focus. This common sense view of comparative advantage suggests that nations would do better if they focus on industries where they have a competitive advantage. In other words, nations prosper when they stick to what it is they do best.

Conservatives believe that free-trade policies equate to a pro-trade, pro-growth economy that often result in lifting societal living standards and that protectionist policies reflect an antitrade bias that results in slower economic growth that is likely to lower societal living standards. Conservatives understand that free-trade policies can result in local job displacements but believe that, on the whole, free-trade policies lead to a net increase in jobs.

Progressives see protectionism as a nationalist "America First" program to protect local jobs (irrespective of their competitiveness in the world) with few negative consequences, whereas Conservatives see protectionism as being unable to protect local jobs in the long run and the beginning of trade wars with other nations, likely reducing the economic output of all participating countries. In other words, noncompetitive industries and jobs will eventually be replaced by competitive industries and jobs, and domestic "Buy American" policies will soon result in foreign "Don't Buy American" policies from our former trading partners. Conservatives see any short-term, local, job-retention advantages from protectionist policies as being offset by long-term disadvantages in price, quality, and selection to American consumers. For example, when the current administration eliminated our agreement with Mexico to allow them certain trucking rights, America's supply-chain costs rose an estimated $8.4 billion a year.

For political and/or provincial reasons, Progressives (the "if we are nice to them, they will be nice to us" crowd and the "if other nations don't like us, it is probably due to some ill-considered or ill-advised American policy" group) who support better relations with allies and even rogue nations around the world cannot see the contradiction in putting up international trade barriers that might start international trade wars. These are the same people who are willing to cede certain sovereign rights to international organizations such as the anti-American United Nations in the name of "transnationalism" and peace. Protectionism just does not make sense for our country. For that matter, neither does transnationalism.

Protectionism allows business to be driven by political concerns rather than economic concerns. This is a bad idea. It is tough enough to start and operate a successful business when focused on customers, suppliers, employees, market forces, innovation, and competitors. It is impossible to operate successfully when the primary focus is political. As stated earlier, protectionist policies drive up consumer prices for necessities (e.g., food, clothing, and shelter). This hurts the middle- and lower-income earners most because they pay a larger percentage of their budget for these items. When the government gives to one constituency, it must first take from another. Ironically, in the case of protectionism, both constituencies (blue-collar workers and lower- or middle-income workers) who lose in this transaction are perceived to be wards of the Progressives.

Why would Progressives not favor free trade? Free trade is opposed, and protectionism is supported using three basic rationalizations: economic, moral, and political. The political argument is based on such slogans and rhetoric as "buy American" and, more recently, "fair trade." "Fair trade" and "buy American" are liberal code words designed to gain populist appeal and support for protectionism. Protectionism is a political and economic philosophy or policy used by unions and management to restrain international trade by imposing duties or quotas on foreign imports in an attempt to protect local industries from foreign competition.

Some politically based arguments against free-trade policies and agreements center around their potential negative impact on national security. The "national security" argument is valid for some industries, but it has often been overused by others (e.g., the watchmaking industry, which actually claimed that they were a vital component of national security) that are not related to national defense or domestic security. Conservatives agree that when national security is at stake, as it might be with certain defense, oil, or even steel-producing industries, some protection to keep these industries alive and well and under U.S. control on U.S. soil is warranted.

Unfortunately most of the politically based arguments against free trade are not founded on the issue of national security. Most are driven by political motivations regarding concerns for reelection. When an elected official represents a district or state with a substantial number of union members or large number of companies that are not competitive with their international competitors, many politicians become focused on only the specific local consequences of free trade and, therefore, oppose it. This kind of opposition might not be in the national interest, but it is understandable given the financial and organizational support (to the local politicians) from these organizations and the focus by many politicians on getting reelected. Regrettably, the balance between supporting local political constituents and doing what is best for the nation is often blurred.

The moral arguments against free trade often focus on issues such as child labor, forced labor, or foreign-employee working conditions. Let me address the issues of child and forced labor first. Conservatives agree that child and forced labor need to be stopped. Anyone who does not see the injustice of these practices is living in a different world. The United States funds several international programs to end these abuses. One is the International Program for the Elimination of Child Labor; this program alone gets $30 million a year from the United States. In fact, no civilized person, Liberal or Conservative, supports child or forced labor.

Liberals and Conservatives agree that all products produced in this manner should be immediately boycotted.

The unfair or less-than-humane treatment of foreign workers is a much more complex issue. Again, no reasonable person supports poor or abusive working conditions, no matter where they reside. However, many of the people enduring these indignities require these jobs for their own subsistence and to support their families. And we know that in some cases, as bad as the current working conditions are, the poor conditions represent improvements over their former working conditions.

Should we stop doing business with these nations and risk increasing the poverty and bad working conditions under which they now live? This is a tough question, and I am not sure that I know the right answer for each situation. The question is not whether or not the free-traders or the protectionists support these abuses; they are against them. The question is whether increasing or decreasing trade with these nations will help to remedy these foul practices or facilitate the continuation of them. Conservatives generally believe our response to poor working conditions might be better judged on a case-by-case basis, whereas proven abuses in child or forced labor should be cause for immediate cessation of trade with the offenders.

The economic arguments by Progressives are much less convincing than the national security argument that can be dealt with on an individual company or industry basis or with the moral arguments for which remedies are not always so clear. The economic concerns Liberals point to usually relate to keeping jobs in the United States, allowing too much money to go to foreign nations, or the "dumping" of goods in America.

As to the issue of "keeping jobs in the United States," most economists would suggest that keeping productive jobs where we are efficient and competitive is more important. But this again is a difficult decision for the local politician. For example, we can examine the auto-manufacturing industry. The loss to foreign competition of ten thousand auto-manufacturing jobs is devastating. The negative impact on the displaced workers and their families outweighs the savings and increases in quality or selection gained by U.S. consumers buying superior foreign cars. On the other hand, because global markets are flourishing, competition from foreign manufacturers provides incentives for U.S. manufacturers to improve, and free-trade policies generally increase the economic output of all nations participating. In the long run, the United States will not be able to survive with isolationist policies; protectionist regulations and laws will only ensure that U.S. companies will not remain competitive with their foreign counterparts.

Again, the question here is not whether free-trade policies will cause local disruptions and displacements. Everyone agrees that they will. The question is, "What is the best way to deal with these negative impacts on local communities?" The Progressive view is to take the short-term advantage of protectionism even though there will be long-term negative consequences that will likely destroy the domestic industry anyway and do eventual harm to the local communities. The Conservative view is to deal compassionately with those who may be displaced while accepting the reality that certain local jobs will be lost to technology, to other more productive domestic competitors, to innovation, to mistakes by management and workers, to changes in domestic preferences and needs, and to foreign competitors with comparative advantages. Conservatives believe that these jobs cannot be protected and saved in the long term from all of these vulnerabilities. The real issues are related to the innovations needed to make our domestic enterprises more competitive and how to soften the blow and ease the transition for those whose jobs were lost.

As to the "money to foreign nations" argument, this is a sixteenth- and seventeenth-century argument of mercantilism. Mercantilism held that exports needed to be encouraged and imports needed to be discouraged. It was thought that these practices would allow gold or other forms of currency to be kept at home, thereby making the net exporter more financially secure. However, very few, if any, current economists support the mercantilist philosophy. The United States needs to promote exports to increase domestic production and income, not for the purpose of hoarding money. When this domestic income is spent on imports, it generally creates an advantage for consumers. The way to promote exports is not by limiting imports with artificial government restrictions. It is by making a better and more desirable product, not by outlawing or handicapping better foreign products and hurting domestic consumers.

As to the charge of "dumping," this practice is already illegal. Dumping occurs when a foreign nation sells its products at a lower price in the United States than it does in its home market. This illegal concept is designed to use the foreign nation's lower-than-cost pricing to put domestic producers out of business and raise prices afterward. This is obviously an unethical as well as illegal practice and would not be allowed by virtue of any free-trade agreement.

An attempt to level the playing field by subsidizing a U.S. industry is really a tax on U.S. consumers. These practices only prolong the death of an obsolete or noncompetitive industry. Liberals often perpetuate the myth of "the race to the bottom" in dealing with the issue of free trade. The Progressive moral argument is that the effects of free trade might help the economy but hurt the environment, might help to exploit child labor, or might promote poverty sweatshops. Free trade is not "a race to the bottom." In fact, free trade is the exact opposite. As goods and services are sold into developing nations, incomes increase and a more vibrant middle class is formed. With increased monies and a more politically powerful middle class, foreign governments have more and more incentives to conform to international standards and greater resources to devote to improving the environment and improving working conditions. Many facts support the notion that in countries where the middle classes grow, so grows the expectations of their quality of life. This factor adds a new political dynamic that positively impacts the way foreign governments regulate businesses.

Imports do not cause a net loss of jobs in this country. Some workers get displaced, but as stated earlier, job losses occur due to many other business and economic factors. Free trade benefits all society, just as technology does. Free trade, like technology-based innovations, does cause some resources to shift to more productive businesses, but it more often than not raises living standards for all. It is always unfortunate and extremely stressful when any worker loses his job, but these displacements cannot be eliminated in a global market and a free society. Perhaps there is an argument here for better retraining facilities, improved community colleges, and more unemployment support to help ease the transition for those who have lost their jobs, but there is not a valid argument here for protectionist or anti-free-trade policies. The displaced individuals need to be supported, but the nation must also remain competitive.

Look at the census of jobs of 1960 and the census of jobs of 2008. Many of the jobs of 1960 do not even exist today and many of the jobs of 2008 had not even been imagined in 1960. Should we have stayed with 1960 products? Would our lives be better without fax machines, cell phones, computers, iPods, Google search engines, or the Internet? Who can say? What we can say, though, is that no amount of restricting the marketplace could have succeeded. The market cannot be legislated out of existence through protectionist measures or any other government policies unless we completely isolate our country (like North Korea) and do away with Free-Market Capitalism. In the long run, free trade will prevail not because it represents a key Conservative value, but because it is good for America.

Principle 7: Fiscal Responsibility

Conservatives Believe in Fiscal Responsibility, an Important Principle and Value within Capitalism.

Operating with fiscal responsibility requires that an individual, a business, or an organization (even one as large as the U.S. government) wisely manage its resources and live within its means by setting priorities, controlling spending, limiting debt, and planning for future needs.

I recently heard the governor of Texas respond to a reporter's question regarding how Texas has remained more fiscally sound than many other states when Texas has no state tax and a part-time state legislature. I suspect his answer was too straightforward and too simple for the average elected politician to understand. When asked, "Why does Texas thrive while California flounders?" he said, "Don't spend all the money." This seems to me as good a place as any to begin our discussion on fiscal responsibility.

Of course, there is more to fiscal responsibility than simply not spending all of the money; however, the issue is not that much more complex. Living within your means is something we all learn at a very young age. So why is it that politicians have not learned it? Why is it that we have out-of-control spending, high national debt, and high federal deficits if the people, the legislature, and the president all want to not have them? Can we blame it all on the high costs of unexpected wars and other national emergencies? I don't think so. Can we blame it on uneducated legislatures and executive branch ignorance? While that is a tempting thought, I doubt it. Did our politicians really not know that their cost estimates of entitlement programs and other spending measures were low? I suspect the opposite is true. They knew they were low, and many wanted to hide the fact from the American people. So is it that the American people did not understand that the country was over-spending its resources? Were our eyes just bigger than our pocketbooks? Were our politicians more interested in buying votes that fiscal responsibility? These last three points have some validity. Many in American society judge the viability of a pending spending measure with a very narrow focus: Will it help me and mine? And will it do some good? Plus, the budget, the deficit, and the debt numbers are so high (trillions of dollars) that politicians can easily hide political favors, and the amount of money involved cannot be comprehended.

Don't Spend More Than You Make

Set Priorities; There Are Not Unlimited Resources
in Your Family or in the Government

*It is incumbent on every generation to pay its own debts
as it goes. A principle which if acted on would save
one-half the wars of the world.*

—Thomas Jefferson

Did our elected politicians not understand the five basic rules of fiscal responsibility?

1. Don't spend more than you make.
2. Don't borrow more than you can repay.
3. Don't print so much new money that the currency is devalued.
4. Don't tax achievers so much that they lose the incentive to achieve.
5. Plan and save for a rainy day.

Again, nearly everyone in power knew these axioms and understood their importance. The answer to the question of how and why we got into this fiscal mess can be explained with five simple facts:

1. Limited Resources. There is little or no understanding in America that even an organization as large as the U.S. government has limited resources. Therefore, there are always more "good" things to do than there are resources to do them. The government can tax only so much until the level of taxation changes the behavior of those being taxed. Sooner or later, excessive taxes generate diminishing returns. The government can borrow only so much until it becomes a bad credit risk. And the government can print only so much currency until the currency devalues and inflation prevails.

2. Priorities. Our political leaders and the American public have never dedicated the time and energy to set priorities. The

Don't tax achievers so much that they lose the incentive to achieve.

fact that resources are limited requires that every organization set priorities whether at the family, the business, or the government level. How will an organization or a family decide what to fund and what not to fund, determine what it can afford and what it cannot afford, or choose how to allocate any of its resources without first setting priorities? Sadly when it comes to government allocations of resources, we know the answer to these questions. We will decide these fiscal matters the way we have for generations: by political clout and deception.

3. Performance Measurement. Our government never determined how to measure the performance (i.e., effectiveness and efficiency) of each of the many programs it sponsors. In large part, this might be because our politicians do not want the American public to have clear performance metrics. With no clear way to measure how well a particular program has performed, there is no corresponding way to measure how well the sponsoring politician has performed. On the other hand, even on the rare occasion when clear performance metrics have been established or when success or failure has become self-evident in spite of having no objective measurements, very few politicians have been held accountable. When the "War on Poverty" program (welfare) was established by Lyndon Baines Johnson, he said that its success would be measured by the reduction of people in poverty and the reduction in the number of people dependent on the government. Both these performance metrics showed terrible failings of the program, but there was little consequence to this failure. When the government sponsored enterprises (GSEs) of Fannie Mae and Freddie Mac failed, those politicians and bureaucrats responsible for the failure completely escaped any consequences. This has to change, and

You rub my back; I'll rub yours.

Compromise: You vote for mine, and I will vote for yours with OPM.

only the American public can force these changes. The first job of our president needs to be to ensure that our country is safe, but the second job needs to be to ensure that our nation is focused on and funding the right issues.

4. Vote-buying. Politicians have learned how to buy votes by providing their constituents with favors (favorable legislation, tax breaks, government jobs, government contracts, or local projects) using other people's money (OPM). This legal but often unethical practice places provincial and reelection concerns in front of what is good for the country. We have heard of bridges to nowhere, Murtha-land airports, and even large government contracts given to friends and relatives, but these examples represent only the tip of the iceberg. This practice is so widespread that we now are all familiar with its name: earmarks. I was surprised that so many earmarks (something like nine thousand in just the first omnibus bill of 2009) were put in the legislation literally in the middle of the night or at times even after voting for the bill was completed. This surprised me not because I saw examples of politicians acting unethically—Who doesn't expect this?—but because we all know that no one who votes for these bills even reads them. So if no one reads them, why the middle-of-the-night chicanery? Legislators have developed many ways to deceive the American public; earmarks are least among them. They produce bills of more than one thousand pages and pass them with no public or political representative scrutiny. The U.S. Tax Code now reaches nearly seventy thousand pages. No one voting on the tax code reads this either. Plus, the sheer size of these documents allows politicians to hide special favors to their supporters, campaign contributors, and constituencies. Legislators often use misleading titles on these bills because they know that only the title will be read. They tack on completely unrelated amendments to important measures to hide the fact they are there. They call the game they play "compromise," but what they often mean is "you vote for mine and I will vote for yours" without regard to their own principles or the value to the country. These huge pieces of legislation are sold with carefully polled and parsed rhetoric designed to hide weaknesses and exaggerate strengths. Often, vague language is used as a gift to trial lawyers. As they say, the devil is in the details, but the details are seldom revealed until the vulture attorneys share them in court.

5. Size of Government. Legislative deception aside, the magnitude of government spending has become so large that even a number as large as a billion dollars is often treated as a rounding error.

Government is not the solution; it is the problem.

If it moves, tax it. If it keeps moving, regulate it.
And if it stops moving, subsidize it.

Government has just grown too big. In business good managers will correct the situation even if only one dollar is misspent. They know that even this small infraction sets the wrong tone for business. Obviously this does not happen in government. Government does things the founders never intended. All three branches of government have contributed, if not conspired, to continually expand the role of government. When a government program is established, it usually goes on forever. Legislators can vote themselves money, privileges, and perks, and they do. Someday I would like to see an accounting of all the benefits of representatives and senators—not just salary, but also all of the laws from which they have exempted themselves, all of the budgets they control, retirement plans, appointments they can make, junkets they are allowed to take, gifts they are allowed to accept, and everything else. How many elected officials have gone into office with a limited net worth but have come out as multimillionaires? For fiscal responsibility to prevail, government must be limited. Too many people are now dependent on government support.

You cannot legislate the poor into freedom by legislating the wealthy out of freedom. What one person receives without working for, another person must work for without receiving. The government cannot give to anybody anything that the government does not first take from somebody else. When half of the people get the idea that they do not have to work because the other half is going to take care of them, and when the other half gets the idea that it does no good to work because somebody else is going to get what they work for, that my dear friend, is about the end of any nation. You cannot multiply wealth by dividing it.

—Adrian Rogers, 1948

This might seem obvious to all but our politicians, but the government cannot borrow its way out of debt. Here are some facts about our government debt:

The Outstanding Public Debt as of June 24, 2009, at 02:46:08 AM GMT (the date of this early draft) is:

$11,405,188,166,362.79

The estimated population of the United States as of June 24, 2009 is **306,423,489;** each citizen's share of this debt is:

$37,220.35

Less than eight months later (at the time of this latest draft), February 15, 2010 at 05:50:29 PM GMT, the Outstanding Public Debt stood at:

$12,364,073,777,735.89

The estimated population of the United States as of February 15, 2010 is **307,845,009** so each citizen's share of this debt is:

$40,163.31

The national debt has continued to increase an average of **$3.85 billion per day** since September 28, 2007!

Check out the U.S. National Debt Clock at **www.usdebtclock. org.**

According to Goldman Sachs Group, Inc., the United States will sell $3.25 trillion of debt in the fiscal year ending September 30, 2009. As of this same date, the nation's marketable debt stood at an unprecedented $6.45 trillion. If we continue to increase government spending, we will be walking far down the path that leads away from Capitalism and into Socialism.

Socialism is a philosophy of failure, the creed of ignorance, and the gospel of envy; its inherent virtue is the equal sharing of misery.

—Winston Churchill

The problem with Socialism is that you eventually run out of other people's money.

—Margaret Thatcher

To cure the British disease with socialism was like trying to cure leukaemia with leeches.

—Margaret Thatcher

The following comments on government have been said often, but are worth repeating and considering. *Government cannot help someone without hurting someone else. It cannot give to someone without first taking from someone else. The government does not create wealth; it only consumes it or redistributes it.*

I love these comments and ideas from the noted economist Dr. Thomas Sowell:

"Elections should be held on April 16th—the day after we pay our income taxes. That is one of the few things that might discourage politicians from being big spenders."
"It is hard to imagine a more stupid or more dangerous way of making decisions than by putting those decisions in the hands of people who pay no price for being wrong."
"Balanced budget requirements seem more likely to produce accounting ingenuity than genuinely balanced budgets."

With continued spending by the government that outpaces its revenue and with continued fiscal irresponsibility, interest and tax rates will be raised, inflation will increase, and government borrowing will crowd out private borrowing. Entrepreneurs and businesses need to be able to find affordable sources of money to fund their enterprises. Because it is so true, the following adage from Ronald Reagan is no longer that funny: ***If it moves, tax it. If it keeps moving, regulate it. And if it stops moving, subsidize it.*** There are now so many taxes that an attempt to list them all would take more pages than are in this whole book. Suffice it to say that the government has become so good at taxing that none of us really understands all the taxes we actually pay. It's not just state and federal income taxes or Social Security tax; there are import tariffs, gas taxes, occupancy taxes, capital gains taxes, alternative minimum taxes (just in case you didn't pay enough other taxes), sales taxes, corporate or business taxes, gift taxes, estate (or death) taxes, and more—many, many more. In addition there are hundreds, if not thousands, of government fees and charges for everything from toll roads to the post office to fishing licenses. This is what you get with an ever-expanding, out-of-control government.

My reading of history convinces me that most bad government results from too much government.

—Thomas Jefferson

Nearly every politician talks of simplifying our tax code, but even as they are saying this to the public, their staffs are working on new ways to tax us. I suspect that our tax code might never be simplified because that would expose or eliminate all of the favors and hidden taxes. The Progressives in the government are looking for more ways to control our lives and to pound us into submission, not more ways to provide individual liberties; the power of taxation presents them with their biggest hammer. It might be important to remember that Liberals often believe that their charter is to redistribute wealth, but they know that the more their methods and plans are exposed, the less likely it will be that the American public will support them. Many actually believe that the government can spend your money more wisely than you can. Therefore, many Progressives consider a long and burdensome tax code to be an advantage.

Who took my money?

The government purposely hides the costs of its future obligations. The kind of "accounting" the government uses would put a businessperson in prison. If a business or a bank modeled its contracts on the tax code—thousands of pages written in code that hides its self-serving fees and other costs—government prosecutors would charge the officers with fraud and be looking for photo ops while they hauled them off to jail. If a businessman runs a Ponzi scheme, as Bernie Madoff did, he is rightfully called a scoundrel and a crook, but if the same man were to have put together such a scheme for government (e.g., Social Security), he would be called a congressman.

In summary, fiscal responsibility is not really a complex subject. Remember the five rules of fiscal responsibility:

1. Don't spend more than you make.
2. Don't borrow more than you can repay.
3. Don't print so much new money that the currency is devalued.
4. Don't tax achievers so much that they lose the incentive to achieve.
5. Plan and save for a rainy day.

America's citizens and its government representatives need to take into account the fact that the resources are limited and, therefore, priorities need to be established. Government program performance needs to be measured, and politicians need to be held accountable. Unethical "vote buying" needs to be exposed and stopped. And government needs to get back to basics and downsize, not grow. With these steps, fiscal responsibility can be reestablished.

Parable #3

"Think Pink"

All through the summer, Tommy and his friends kept finding ways to make their lemonade stand better and better. Benny's sister Rose watched the boys work, and an idea began to take form in her little head. She didn't tell anybody about it, not for a while. But she never stopped thinking about it.

Finally she called up a couple of friends. "Randi, Joanie, it's Rose." And she told them her idea. "Last week, me and Benny were at the fair, and I got some pink lemonade and it was *so* delicious. And so I started thinking. We could get together and open a pink lemonade stand!"

"That's a fantastic idea!" said Joanie.

"Awesome!" said Randi.

"But," Joanie said then, "where do you get pink lemons?"

"You don't," Rosie explained. "There're different ways to make it, but I like it when you take regular lemonade and add cranberry juice."

"You think the boys will mind?" asked Joanie.

"We can ask 'em," said Rosie.

And they did ask, and Tommy and his friends thought it was a great idea. It'd bring more people to the block for lemonade. It'd be good for *all* of them!

Rosie, Joanie, and Randi asked their friends Ellie, Laurie, and Suzy to help. They built their own stand, right across the street from the boys' place, and painted it sparkly pink. Randi and Laurie made signs, and Ellie brought a big, pink umbrella so their customers could drink in the nice, cool shade. Rosie, Joanie, and Suzy got to work making a few gallons of pink lemonade.

The next day, another hot day, the girls were ready for their grand opening! For the first few hours, nobody came by. And for the next few hours, nobody came. Across the street, the boys had plenty of customers.

But nobody wanted to try that weird pink stuff.

Things were not looking good for Rosie and her friends. In fact, things were looking really bad. They were going to have a lot of leftover lemonade at the end of that day.

But then Laurie had an idea. She saw a kid standing on the sidewalk, afraid to come over and try this new kind of lemonade. Laurie poured a cup and took it to him and said, "Here you go, kid. Free sample. On the house."

The little boy took a teeny, tiny sip of that pink lemonade. Then he tried another short sip. And another. "Man!" he shouted. "This stuff is great!"

The little boy told his friends, and they came by and tried the new kind of lemonade. And they liked it and told their friends.

Before long, the girls had more customers than they could handle. All the new customers brought *more* customers to the block, and *both* lemonade stands were busy!

The moral of the story: Capitalism allows individuals to pursue self-interest while providing benefits to the community.

Note to parents: This story is an analogy of how our economy and our society have prospered through the Capitalist system.

Chapter 10

The Proper Role of Government

Principle 8: Limited Government
Principle 9: Individual Freedom

As the principles portrayed in Chapter 8 and Chapter 9, the primary role of government is to protect the rights of its citizens as detailed in the Constitution, not to grant new rights without going through the constitutional amendment process. Government has an important but limited role to play while it protects us from harm and provides us an atmosphere that supports civil interactions, productivity, and innovation. After the right to life, the right to individual liberty and freedom might be the next most important right; a key constitutional mechanism to protect this right lies in the concept of *limited government*. Although the Constitution does place boundaries on the activities of individuals, of equal or perhaps even more importance is that it specifies what the federal government may do and especially what it may *not* do. In large part, it is the job of the Constitution to protect the freedom of the people from the government.

The laws of our nation allow for limited government intervention in matters of personal liberty and commerce. The Ninth and Tenth Amendments clearly spell out the concept of limited government. The Ninth Amendment established that the rights of people do not

145

have to be expressly written in the Constitution for the people to retain them. This amendment allows for increased individual liberties but also seems to give government some considerable latitude in determining or defining its powers. However, the Tenth Amendment says, *"the powers not delegated to the United States by the Constitution, nor prohibited by it to the States, are reserved to the States respectively, or to the people."* Regrettably, this provision has been weakened by reinterpretations by activist judges and justices or just ignored.

It has been said that all Government is an evil. It would be more proper to say that the necessity of any Government is a misfortune. This necessity however exists; and the problem to be solved is, not what form of government is perfect, but which of the forms is least imperfect.

—James Madison

Citizens Are Free to Pursue Happiness, Life, and Liberty without Undue Government Interference

In today's circumstances there needs to be much more attention, discussion, and education regarding the future of individual
liberty in an environment of an ever-expanding role of government.
The people of the United States, through its founders, established
a limited government to address such matters as the protection of
its citizens, the facilitation of interstate commerce, and the creation
of an environment of equal opportunity. ***The government works
for the people; the people do not work for the government.*** By
their actions and attitudes, this important distinction has apparently escaped many of our elected politicians and the bureaucrats
they appoint.

The notion of individual freedom and liberty reflects a moral
philosophy and social outlook that stresses independence and self-
reliance along with such entitlements as the right to bear arms,
the right to be free from unreasonable searches and seizures, the
right to free speech, and the right to freedom of religion. Liberty
and freedom support the virtues in man, while the government,
through the rule of law, the establishment of regulations, and the
courts and law enforcement, attempts to counteract or control the
vices. Therein lies the paradox. Some government is necessary;
however, the more government, the less individual freedom. And
finding the right balance between the power of government and
liberties of individuals has remained the subject of political debate
for more than two hundred years.

The consensus of our founders, as well as that of Conservatives
today, is that government power must be limited (and now curtailed)
if individual liberty is to exist. The reasons our founding fathers
saw fit to limit the powers of government are set forth candidly and
clearly in the Declaration of Independence, in which they explained
why they were severing their political connections to Great Britain.
The Declaration of Independence set forth three basic premises so

commonly accepted by the people of the time that they were considered "self-evident." As we all know, these self-evident truths included the belief that *all men are created equal, that they are endowed by their Creator with certain unalienable rights, and that government derives all of its powers from and by the consent of the governed.*

The first ten amendments to the U.S. Constitution are called the Bill of Rights. It is generally accepted that the Bill of Rights limits the power of the U.S. government in two ways. First, it restricts the reach and range of government intervention and authority in certain areas such as the individual rights to free speech, freedom of religion, and free association. These individual rights (and others like them) represent areas where the government is not allowed to tread. In other words, the government may not pass laws or set regulations abridging these personal liberties. Second, the Bill of Rights sets forth certain forms or processes the government must follow when interacting with its people (e.g., due process, no unreasonable search or seizure, and no one can be compelled to testify against him- or herself). By this limitation, the government is prevented from treating its citizens arbitrarily or capriciously. In other words, not only the people, but also the government must follow the rule of law.

Below is a brief summary of specific rights retained by the people to safeguard individual liberty and freedom by virtue of the Bill of Rights:

1. Freedom of speech and religion.
2. The right to bear arms.
3. The right not to have soldiers stay in your home without your permission.
4. The right to have no unreasonable searches of self or property.
5. The right to due process of law.

6. The right to a fair and speedy trial.
7. The right to a jury trial.
8. The right to no cruel and unusual punishment.
9. Lack of enumeration in the Constitution does not deny rights.
10. Federal government powers not delegated in the Constitution are reserved for the states and *the people*.

Unfortunately, the government has grown far out of proportion to its responsibilities and obligations, in spite of the founders' intentions to keep it limited. Government officials have become masters at using *other people's money* to fund its disproportionate growth. As legislators honed their skills in "helping" certain citizens by taking from others, more and more people have become dependent on the government. And as more people have become dependent on the government, the government has grown at rates never foreseen. Politicians continue to establish more "rights," and the judiciary has helped by finding new rights for individuals and new obligations for the government that were previously undiscovered for at least 125 years after the Constitution was established. It is estimated 40 to 60 percent of Americans receive some form of compensation or subsistence from the government.

The founders knew they could not predict future circumstances and established a process for amending the Constitution to keep the document relevant to the changing times that lay and lie ahead. However, it appears they badly underestimated the cleverness and ingenuity of people who wanted something for nothing, and the deception and level of self-interest existing in those in government who would help these people achieve their goals. Our founders did not fully anticipate that the people of the United States and their local representatives from the House and Senate would make such blatant efforts to bypass the constitutional amendment process. The founders purposefully made the process of amending the Constitution difficult. A constitutional amendment can be proposed by a vote of two-thirds of Congress or a constitutional convention can be convened for the purpose of proposing amendments with a two thirds vote of the legislatures of the several states . To be passed, a constitutional amendment requires ratification by three-quarters of the states. As of 2009, the most recent amendment is the twenty-seventh, which was ratified in 1992.

Why do Liberals believe in expanded government that results in limited liberty?

Many Liberals believe the Constitution is an outdated document full of "negative liberties" detailing a too-long list of all the things the government should not or cannot do. They see their role as being the catalyst for change. Their goal is to expand government and to establish new rights for old constituencies to correct what they see as societal ills or social injustice. They see themselves as social engineers. Many Progressives believe that they, and only they, can "fix" what the founders got wrong. Liberals believe the Constitution needs to be adapted to the twenty-first century. What they could not and cannot get through constitutional amendment or popular vote, they are now attempting (all too successfully) to get through the courts. The founders intended for the federal courts, including the Supreme Court, to be the nonpolitical branch of government that would protect us from constitutional shortcuts of the kind that Progressives are now exploiting. Lifetime appointments of federal judges and justices were put in place to help preserve the concept of limited government. It is truly unfortunate that this mechanism designed to ensure objectivity has failed so miserably. Throughout the twentieth century, the courts have become filled with those who believe their ideology stands above the law.

As Thomas Jefferson implied in the quote below, the constitutional concept of limited government did not apply to only government authorities; it also applied to the limited rights of individuals.

The policy of the American government is to leave their citizens free, neither restraining nor aiding them in their pursuits.

—Thomas Jefferson

This concept of limited government authority and limited individual rights has become completely lost in the minds of current Progressives. What Progressives are trying to progress away from is the original intent of the Constitution as it was written. They see Conservatives as stuck in the past or as unsympathetic to those in need because Conservatives will support only equal opportunity, not equal outcomes. They feel that Conservative opposition to expanded government support reflects mean-spiritedness or a focus on only the concerns of business or the rich. It does not seem to matter to Progressives that so many government-support programs they have initiated and championed, despite their original good intentions, eventuated into failure. As long as their intentions were good and they were trying to help, they do not seem to mind that their programs of *help* often turned out to be programs of *harm*. Liberals seem not to be fazed by historical evidence that more people in need have been helped and raised out of poverty by Free-Market Capitalism than have ever been helped through big-government central planning.

Like the founding fathers, Conservatives believe that individual freedom is priceless and never goes out of style. For each and every American, everyone is equal under the law. There are no favorites in

*government; justice is blind. And everyone is guaranteed equal oppor-
tunity but not equal outcome.*

Without getting into the major financial failures of Social
Security or Medicare, which are both going broke, take a look at
some of the more innocuous-sounding Liberal government "help"
programs such as *minimum wage* or *rent control.* Minimum wage was
originally intended to help preserve union jobs and increase the
pay of blue-collar workers of minimum skill. However, as Milton
Friedman pointed out more than forty years ago, the minimum-
wage law forced employers to discriminate against any worker
whose skills could not justify the legal minimum wage level set by
the government. This especially increased the level of unemployment of teenagers. Rent control was put in place as a temporary
measure during World War II. But like nearly all government
support programs, it still exists today. Rent control was intended
to make good housing available at affordable prices. However, in
addition to the rampant fraud in this program (there is at least
one Congressman with a rent-controlled apartment), with no
incentive to maintain or improve this housing (because of below-
market fixed-rent income), this housing became run down, often to
the point of being unlivable. Rent control actually made housing
less available and, therefore, less affordable, and minimum wage
continues to promote discrimination toward low-skilled workers
and has certainly not helped union members. In spite of these facts,
Liberals still support them.

It is easy to see why well-meaning sponsors and special-interest
supporters were originally motivated to increase the power and
size of government. Those sponsors were just trying to help, and
the supporters were getting paid off with campaign donations or
political organizational assistance. The special-interest propo-
nents receive reelection for their promotion of these programs.

This practice might not reflect the best character, but it is understandable. However, one would think that the well-meaning but ill-informed sponsors of these programs would recognize the error of their ways once they saw the gap between their good intentions and their poor results. Perhaps there are now just more of the former and fewer of the latter.

It has been said many times that ***a government that is big enough to give you everything you want is big enough to take everything you have.*** This is a thought for all of us to consider.

General Welfare Clause: The Death of Individual Freedom

When the issue of limited government is discussed, especially as it might relate to constitutional authorities and prohibitions, the General Welfare Clause will sooner or later come to the forefront of the conversation.

Article I, Section 8 of the U.S. Constitution grants Congress the power to *"lay and collect taxes, duties, imposts, and excises, to pay the debts and provide for the common defence and general welfare of the United States."* There has been much debate over the past two hundred years or so regarding whether this language gave new and unenumerated powers to the government. Some argued that this clause gave Congress carte blanche to pass any legislation that it pleased so long as its purpose was defined as promotion of the general welfare. Others felt that the notion of new, broad powers to spend for the general welfare gave Congress power over that which it could not regulate directly.

In other words, they argued that a broad interpretation of the General Welfare Clause would undo the limitations placed on Congress by the listing of enumerated powers. In the 1930s the courts ruled on the issue when it considered and sustained the benefits provision of the Social Security Act of 1935. In effect, the court ruled that Congress did have the power to tax and spend under the General Welfare Clause so long as the taxing and spending was done to address national (versus local) concerns. Further, the court said that Congress itself could determine when spending constituted spending for the general welfare. This opened the floodgates to Liberal tax and spenders. There has been no instance to date of legislation being overturned on the grounds of its failure to serve the general welfare.

How is it that the inherent lie of good intentions without corresponding good results has gained so much traction? Perhaps it's because the availability of other people's money to fund these social experiments has been so plentiful. Or could it be that our politicians have become so adept at deception and misrepresentation that too many of us have been fooled by their clever rhetoric? Is it that the mainstream media (network TV and large newspapers) are so in favor of bigger government that biased reporting has given too many of us the wrong perceptions? Could it be that as long as the programs sound compassionate, there are too many people who just don't care which ones are instituted as long as someone else is footing the bill?

The availability of other people's money has been too great. Our politicians and the mainstream media have fooled some of us with clever, incisive sound bites and biased reporting. Plus, there is no doubt that the excessive use of other people's money is impacted by the fact, as reported by CNNMoney.com (September 30, 2009), that nearly half the people in our country do not pay income taxes. *However, the real issue is that of ignorance and complacency that has resulted in citizen apathy.* The four out of ten eligible voters who do not vote (and the likely six out of ten who do vote but are not fully informed) either believe things are all right or that nothing done in the government will have much effect on them. In other words, it appears as if so many people are satisfied with the status quo that they feel no need to participate in our political system.

Status quo, you know, is Latin for "the mess we're in."

—Ronald Reagan

To some degree, we might be victims of our own success. Could it be that too many people are just not worried about the future? To these people, the historical failures of central planning are not relevant in their daily lives. Perhaps they are too busy with other family or business issues, or perhaps they have not given much thought to political philosophy or our country's history as it relates to our liberties and freedoms. The solution, of course, is education.

Over the past several administrations, we've seen that when Liberals are in power, they grow the government at record speed; while Conservatives are in power, they strive to limit the growth of government. From early in the Reagan administration until the year 2000, the size of the federal government relative to the GNP declined by more than 5 percent, dropping from 23.5 percent to 18.4 percent. Spending wasn't reduced, but the economy grew at a faster pace, which provided more breathing room for the private sector. Eight years later, GNP was up a bit; by 2009, it had risen as high as 28 percent.

Even the progressive magazine *Newsweek* ran the title *"We Are All Socialists Now"* on its February 11, 2009, cover. According to *Newsweek*, total government spending in 2010 will be 39.9 percent GNP, only 8 percent below the average in Europe's Socialist countries. Furthermore, according to *Forbes*, the Congressional Budget Office projected that U.S. debt would be 42 percent of GDP in 2019 if Liberals have their way.

Benjamin Franklin questioned, ***"Can we keep the republic?"***

And on the potential for loss of freedom, John Adams and Thomas Jefferson made the following remarks:

But a Constitution of Government once changed from Freedom,
can never be restored. Liberty, once lost, is lost forever.

—John Adams
Letter to Abigail Adams, July 17, 1775

---

*The natural progress of things is for liberty
to yield and government to gain ground.*

—Thomas Jefferson
Letter to Edward Carrington, May 27, 1788

*When the people fear their government, there is tyranny;
when the government fears the people, there is liberty.*

—Thomas Jefferson

Government growth equals more government corruption and more government inefficiency. As they say, power corrupts, and when the government grows, it accumulates power. In addition, when the government enters the private sector, it creates extraordinarily expensive jobs (typically for the cost of each of these government-created jobs, the government could have paid the worker more than the job paid and required the "worker" to do nothing for the rest of his life). The federal government is the largest single employer in the United States. According to a January 29, 2010, Pat Buchanan article at Townhall.com, "At the local, state, and federal level, there are 19 million to 20 million government employees."

Government jobs of any kind are seldom productive. This is not because of any flaw in the people working in government; it is the political concerns driving government-sponsored organizations, the lack of a system that measures and rewards success (often for politically correct reasons), the excessive demands of government-employee unions for unproductive work rules and above-market compensation, and the watchdog mentality that creates massive bureaucracy. Government job productivity pales against comparable private-sector job productivity. When you want a package to get somewhere by tomorrow morning, do you use the U.S. Postal Service or FedEx?

Governments tend not to solve problems, only to rearrange them.

—Ronald Reagan

Freedom is never more than one generation away from extinction. We didn't pass it to our children in the bloodstream. It must be fought for, protected, and handed on for them to do the same.

—Ronald Reagan

What are the real problems when the government expands and grows too much?

- It is easier to hide favors for potential voters and campaign contributors. For example, the legislature can pass a thousand-page bill without reading it and add three hundred pages in the middle of the night on the eve of the vote all on climate change or global warming or whatever they are calling the massive spending.
- The expansion dilutes attention to what the government should be doing. Like every organization, when the government loses focus, efficiency and effectiveness deteriorate.
- The government will grow beyond its means and will tax too much, borrow too much, and print too much currency.
- The government crowds out private enterprise and individuals in the debt market. The government competes for available credit and creates shortages; therefore, money becomes less available and more expensive for everyone.
- There is excessive concentration of power, wealth, and prestige that often leads to increased corruption. The greater the

power to be had, the greater the competition for the authority to control that power.

- The government expands by confiscating the earnings of private citizens. The government does not earn its money; it only transfers money from the people who have earned it.
- When government expands, individual liberty contracts.

It will be of little avail to the people that the laws are made by men of their own choice if the laws be so voluminous that they cannot be read, or so incoherent that they cannot be understood.

—James Madison

The Constitution begins with "We the People of the United States"; it does not begin with "We the Monarchy" or "We the Government." The words *We the People* imply voluntary cooperative action. These words assume that the formation of some level of government reflects the aggregate needs of the people and no more. Too much of the world already lives under a heavy hand of governmental rule. Those who support a greater level of collectivism and government control have failed to learn the lessons of history. Throughout history, nearly all people have lived under totalitarian repression, tyranny, and misery. Obviously this is where human nature can take us again if we are not diligent.

Those who believe in government benevolence seem to feel that transferring power to the government will make life better for those in need because they think they will be transferring power away from selfish and greedy individuals. History tells a much different story. There are no fewer greedy and selfish individuals in government than there are in the private sector. There are no philosopher-kings, as Plato envisioned, and there are no angels here on Earth to lead our government.

Our country prospers when we allow our people, with minimal restraints, to be the masters of their own destinies. The people actually can spend their money more wisely than the government can. We cannot rely alone on constitutional protections or divisions of power among the branches of government to protect our liberties. For it is not the government from which the Constitution is protecting us; it is "We the People" who must be controlled. The Constitution appears to protect us from a too-strong central government, but it is actually protecting us from a too-strong majority. We the people have rights given to us by our Creator, but we can keep them only if we learn from history and carefully set the boundaries of power for everyone. We must engage in the political process and diligently protect our liberties from those who would take them from us.

Parable #4

"Making a Stand for the Stand"

As that summer rolled on, the days kept getting longer and hotter. And both the lemonade stands kept doing great business. Pretty much everybody in town seemed to stop by for lemonade once or twice a day.

Tommy and his friends and Rosie and her friends got right to work, early each morning, mixing their gallons of lemonade, baking cookies and muffins and what have you. Then, as the day started to warm up, they'd open their stands, and the customers would come. After a while it got to be a routine. Those kids could've done it in their sleep.

And that's almost what happened. I'm sorry to say the kids got a little bit lazy. Tommy, John, Benny, Roger, and Robbie and Rosie, Joanie, Randi, Ellie, Laurie, and Suzy started taking it all for granted. You can hardly blame the kids, things were going so well.

Both stands had happy customers and plenty of them.

And that's what made the mayor take notice. He saw the stands, and he saw the crowds every day as he drove home for lunch with his wife, Mildred. And he started thinking, *Those kids must be raking in some serious money.*

That afternoon the mayor had a little talk with his city council. "You've all seen those lemonade stands across town?"

"Oh, sure!" said one of the councilmen. "I stop by there every day, at least once a day."

"I was by there at lunchtime," said a councilwoman.

"I bet those kids are raking in some serious money," said the mayor.

And the city council agreed, yep, they probably were. And wasn't this city lucky to have young people like that?

"If *they're* making money," the mayor went on, "then *we* should be making money."

The city council members didn't say anything to this. They weren't sure what he was talking about.

"Taxes!" the mayor shouted. "I'm talking about taxes! Permits! We can use that money to pay for all kinds of things! The kind of things that make voters like us and vote for us!"

"Oh!" said the city council members. Now they saw what he meant.

By the end of that day, the mayor and the council had come up with dozens of new taxes, permits, fees, regulations, rules, and such.

And the next morning, as soon as the lemonade stands opened, the mayor was there with a stack of papers for the kids.

"What's this, sir?" asked Tommy.

"Just a few things you children need to take care of," said the mayor as he gave another pile of pages to Rosie and her friends. "Taxes, permits, fees, regulations, rules, and such."

The kids took the paperwork home to show their parents. Tommy's mom was shocked, and Rosie's dad was too. The city was asking for taxes and back taxes, a half dozen permits, a dozen new fees, and rent money from the stands.

Now these kids knew they had to pay their fair share of taxes once they made enough to owe some taxes. But the city was trying to take a lot more than they'd ever expected. There was no way they could afford all these taxes, fees, and permits. There was no way they could stay in business.

And so the next morning, at the start of another scorching day, the lemonade stands did not open.

The crowds came just the same, and people waited in long lines. Even two of the city council members came by for a cup of lemonade. But the stands never did open. And the people went thirsty for all that long, hot day.

When word got around about what happened—about the taxes, fees, permits, and such—the townsfolk were furious. They made signs and they marched around city hall, shouting, "Don't take our lemonade stand!"

Inside, the mayor and his city council watched out the window.

"They don't look too happy," said a councilwoman.

"And they don't look too likely to vote for us," said a councilman.

The mayor refused to admit that his plan had backfired. But the city council members told him to drop the taxes, fees, permits, and such.

"Or else," they added.

"Or else what?" he asked.

"Or else we go out there and march with 'em," said the council members.

The mayor got the point then. The taxes, fees, permits, and such were dropped, and the lemonade stands opened once again.

The moral of the story: Big government policies and programs don't build a strong, prosperous nation; free enterprise, individual liberties, and limited government authority are the key.

Note to parents: This story is about the dangers of becoming complacent when our elected officials try to execute noble-sounding objectives by putting undue burdens on citizens. Our founders believed in limited government authority and maximum individual liberties. They understood the power of entrepreneurs.

Chapter 11

The Keystones of Conservatism

Principle 10: Personal Responsibility
Principle 11: Moral Character and Values

Personal responsibility and moral character are the glue that ensures the unalienable rights that our founders envisioned in our country's founding documents. Our nation cannot protect the country, the society, or its own rights with a disinterested, uninvolved, uninformed, immoral, amoral, or corrupt citizenry. Our country was founded on the concept that ordinary people with common sense and upstanding moral character can make good decisions for themselves. The whole concept of rugged individualism and Capitalist entrepreneurism assumes that millions and millions of American citizens will make better decisions for themselves than the government can make for them.

A man does what he must, in spite of personal consequences,
in spite of obstacles and dangers and pressures,
and that is the basis of all human morality.

—John F. Kennedy

Do the Right Thing

Personal responsibility and moral character require courage, individualism, personal honor, personal morality, clear understanding of right and wrong, and recognition that hard work and dedication affect personal success. If individuals are to be responsible for their own circumstances, honesty, good behavior, and hard work need to become part of their character. In other words, while pursuing self-interest to do well, some significant percentage of society also needs to be focused on doing good. Fortunately, our founding fathers understood that laying a moral foundation for the nation not only helped them personally, but also established an environment that generated benefits for all in society. Their effort to establish the economic structure of Capitalism and rule of law found in our Constitution provides considerable help in achieving the opportunity for prosperity for all.

Moral cowardice that keeps us from speaking our minds is as dangerous to this country as irresponsible talk. The right way is not always the popular and easy way. Standing for right when it is unpopular is a true test of moral character.

—Margaret Chase Smith, American senator

Principle 10: Personal Responsibility

The Importance of Personal Responsibility

The whole concept of self-reliance, personal responsibility, and moral character is the oil in the machine that makes our American political and Capitalist system work. With every right given to us by our Creator, there comes a corresponding element of responsibility. We the people can rely on the insights of our founders for only so much; for the rest of our needs, we must rely on personal responsibility and character. The Constitution was designed to protect us from ourselves, and Capitalism allows us to provide societal benefits while pursuing self-interest. But these elements alone are not enough to safeguard our liberties or to keep our country strong and prosperous. Sooner or later human nature and individual ingenuity will find a way around our legal and structural defenses. As we see all too often today, people soon learn how to beat any safeguard and to game any system of checks and balances. It is up to the people of our nation to exercise their personal responsibility to ensure that government works properly as it was designed. Without that diligence, it won't.

Today we see more and more people using the government to take what they know others have earned. It is right for the disabled, the victims of catastrophes, and the truly needy to expect help. Further, it is our responsibility as a compassionate nation to take care of those who cannot take care of themselves. However, many citizens who can fend for themselves but choose not to have become accustomed to government assistance. Individual responsibility occurs when we hold ourselves accountable for our own choices and decisions. Prosperity is possible when ordinary people are allowed to unleash their energy and innovation. Prosperity is likely when the innovation of millions of people solves millions of problems while exploring millions of opportunities. In most cases, the government needs to get out of the way and let good people make this natural process happen.

In the following quote, Benjamin Franklin was a bit too harsh and a bit too unsympathetic to the truly helpless. However, his point about making people "easy in poverty" has some validity. Men and women of good heart will differ on this issue, but it is our responsibility to take care of the helpless, not to take care of those who are capable but merely choose not to take care of themselves.

---

*I am for doing good to the poor, but I differ in opinion of the means. I think the best way of doing good to the poor, is not making them easy **in** poverty, but leading or driving them **out** of it. In my youth I travelled much, and I observed in different countries, that the more public provisions were made for the poor, the less they provided for themselves, and of course became poorer.*

And, on the contrary, the less was done for them,
the more they did for themselves, and became richer.

There is no country in the world where so many provisions are
established for them; so many hospitals to receive them when they
are sick or lame, founded and maintained by voluntary charities;
so many alms-houses for the aged of both sexes, together
with a solemn general law made by the rich to subject
their estates to a heavy tax for the support of the poor.

Under all these obligations, are our poor modest, humble, and
thankful; and do they use their best endeavors to maintain
themselves, and lighten our shoulders of this burden? On the
contrary, I affirm that there is no country in the world in which the
poor are more idle, dissolute, drunken, and insolent.

The day you passed that act, you took away from before their eyes
the greatest of all inducements to industry, frugality, and sobriety,
by giving them a dependence on somewhat else than a careful
accumulation during youth and health, for support in age or sickness.

In short, you offered a premium for the encouragement
of idleness, and you should not now wonder that it has had
its effect in the increase of poverty.

—Benjamin Franklin, "The Encouragement of Idleness," 1776

Perhaps it would be helpful to consider the notions of Benjamin Franklin when we attempt to help those in need or listen to Ronald Reagan when he said, **"We should measure welfare's success by how many people leave welfare, not by how many are added."**

Ordinary people of sound mind and compassionate heart understand the times when help is truly warranted and other times when "tough love" might be the solution. Somehow the process of being elected to office appears to have diminished the faculties of those elected to the point where these distinctions can no longer be made. Without the engagement of honest people, politicians will seldom, if ever, find the courage and fortitude to eliminate a government assistance program they once supported. It is the nature of politicians to be this way, and it will take the character and engagement of average citizens to get them to change.

But what is government itself but the greatest of all reflections on human nature? If men were angels, no government would be necessary. If angels were to govern men, neither external nor internal controls on government would be necessary. In framing a government which is to be administered by men over men, the great difficulty lies in this: you must first enable the government to control the governed; and in the next place, oblige it to control itself. A dependence on the people is, no doubt, the primary control on the government; but experience has taught mankind the necessity of auxiliary precautions.

—James Madison (suspected author)
The Federalist Papers, No. 51

It is difficult for the people to meet James Madison's challenge to control the government when nearly half of the governed are accepting subsidy from that government. When the capable take from the government, they are stealing from the incapable. Dealing with this issue alone will fully test the character of our citizenry.

Why do Progressives attempt to ignore the importance of personal responsibility and diminish our sense of moral character?

Unlike Conservatives, Liberals appear to have doubts that average people can be self-sufficient and self-reliant. It seems that many in the Progressive wing feel ordinary citizens can be trusted neither to spend their own money wisely nor to make good decisions for themselves. Liberal policies often reflect the view that a significant number of average people in our nation require governmental assistance, guidance, and regulations to protect them from themselves and from society and its everyday hurdles. Chronic reliance on government support has the side effect of relieving many recipients of feeling any sense of personal responsibility for their circumstances. Once personal responsibility is abandoned, it becomes easier for otherwise capable people to take on the role of victim. This might, in part, be a factor in why often as many as two or three generations within some families and some whole neighborhoods fall into a cycle of dependency and remain on the public dole for decades.

I sincerely, then, believe with you in the general existence of a moral instinct. I think it the brightest gem with which the human character is studded, and the want of it as more degrading than the most hideous of the bodily deformities.

—Thomas Jefferson to Thomas Law, June 13, 1814

Personal responsibility occurs only when personal accountability is accepted. Blame is often cast on others when personal choices go wrong. Fast-food chains are often blamed for the high obesity rates in the United States even though no one is forced to eat at one. Big oil and natural gas companies are blamed for high oil and gas prices and for U.S. dependence on foreign oil, while personal conservation is weak and the government refuses to develop and exploit domestic oil and gas reserves, nuclear power, or clean coal technologies.

As stated by many, *"Personal responsibility is both liberty's reward and price."*

Consequences and Dangers of Making Bad Choices

Life is about choices, and whether the decision is to participate or not to participate in any process of association, a choice is made. For example, when a person chooses bad friends, he or she has chosen to take a certain risk. As the saying goes, "Show me your friends, and I will show you your future." Whether it is with friends or foes, with or without an audience, we all have an obligation to

Not My Fault

We seem to be moving steadily in the direction of a society where no one is responsible for what he himself did but we all are responsible for what somebody else did, either in the present or in the past.
—*Thomas Sowell*

support good behavior and to condemn bad behavior. As we all know, character is often revealed when no one is looking.

We define character as the sum of those qualities of moral excellence that stimulate a person to do the right thing, which is manifested through right and proper actions despite internal or external pressures to the contrary.

—U.S. Air Force Academy

Principle 11: Moral Character and Values

Moral Relativism and Moral Equivalence

Whenever someone says, "The other side has done worse," "Everybody is doing it," or "Others in my place have acted similarly," suspect moral relativism. Right is right and wrong is wrong. It is illogical and deceptive to attempt to rationalize bad actions by bringing up similar or greater wrongdoings of others. If the act is wrong, a greater wrongdoing by others is irrelevant. Another polemic tactic is that of moral equivalence. Moral equivalence occurs when someone attempts to rationalize wrongdoing and to diminish deviance by equating a minor misdeed with a major offense. This deception of semantics was seen and heard recently when the illegal but minor mistreatment of several U.S. POWs was compared to that of suicide or homicide bombers who killed hundreds of innocent civilians.

Personal Responsibility Requires Courage and Sacrifice

Personal responsibility does not come naturally to man. It requires sacrifice and courage to do the right thing. When a baby is born, he is selfish and cries for his wants and needs to be met immediately, no matter what. He knows of no one's welfare but his own. As the baby grows into a toddler and a youth, cultural values are instilled. Toddlers and young children are taught to share, to respect others, and to develop manners. By a certain stage of development, young people know not to hurt others, not to hurt themselves, and not to engage in dangerous activities. This is the beginning of self-reliance and personal responsibility. As these children grow, they are taught the lessons and rewards of moral character. They are taught the lessons of history because their experience has been limited, their capacity to reason has not yet fully matured, and their morality is still under development. **"All that is necessary for the triumph of evil is that good men do nothing."** This statement from Edmund Burke is famous. When logical syllogisms are applied to this thought, it could be stated that when good men do nothing, irresponsibility prevails, or when good men do nothing, corruption prevails. And in the case of the nation, when good men do nothing, their liberties are at risk.

The hottest place in Hell is reserved for those
who remain neutral in times of great moral conflict.

—Martin Luther King, Jr.

Conservatives believe that to protect our nation, our individual rights, and the opportunity for our children to enjoy peace and prosperity, good men and women need to understand the lessons of history and use their reason and sense of morality to evaluate their own experience in order to successfully engage and prevail. It is these eleven principles and the power of *we the people* that are the keys to taking back our country, right here and right now!

Parable #5

"Doing the Right Thing"

The weather stayed hot all through that long July. And in August it got hotter. But no matter how hot it got, the people of Liberty knew they could cool off with a nice, cold cup of lemonade. Tommy and his friends and Rosie and her friends were there at the stands, day after day, ready to help their customers.

One day when it was hotter than hot and even a cup of cold lemonade wouldn't cool you down, Rosie got an idea. She called the other girls together and told them, "We have an ice shaver machine at home, and I think it still works. What if we tried making pink lemonade snow cones?"

Well, all the girls thought that sounded great, especially on a scorching day such as this. That night they all met at Rosie's house and tried making snow cones. The first try was the simplest, pink lemonade poured over shaved ice. It was good, but they knew it could be better. Rosie and her friends kept mixing different ingredients until . . .

"Ooh, ooh, ooh, that's it!" cried Rosie when she tasted the next snow cone.

"Definitely," added Joanie.

"It's perfect," said Ellie.

They wrote down their secret recipe and made plans to meet extra early in the morning.

The next day was hotter than the one before, and Tommy and his friends were selling a lot of lemonade. They could hardly keep up with the crowds. But then along around noon,

Robbie happened to look across the street. "What's goin' on over there?" he wondered.

The rest of the boys looked too, and saw a long line at the girls' stand, stretching half a block. Now Tommy and his friends had plenty of business, but it was nothing like what the girls' had.

Benny went over to find out what was up. He saw everybody ordering pink lemonade snow cones and decided to try one himself.

"The line starts down there," Rosie told him when he tried to cut.

So Benny waited for twenty minutes before he got to taste a pink lemonade snow cone. "This thing's fantastic," he told the guys. "We oughta sell 'em too."

"How do you make 'em?" John asked.

"I don't know," said Benny. "But how hard can it be?"

The boys met that night at Roger's house because Roger had an old ice shaver machine too. They mixed their lemonade with shaved ice, and it was good, but they knew it could be better. They spent hours trying different ingredients, but they never found anything that tasted as good as the girls' pink lemonade snow cones. Benny said he'd ask Rosie about it that night.

And when he asked, "Rosie, what makes your snow cones so good?" she told him, "It's our secret ingredient."

"What's your secret ingredient?" Benny wanted to know.

"If I told you, it wouldn't be secret."

Later that night Benny went to ask her again. "She's not here," said his mom. "She's over at Laurie's house."

Benny went to Rosie's room to look for Laurie's phone number. He picked up his sister's address book, and a small sheet of paper fell out. On it was the girls' recipe. Pomegranate juice—that was the secret ingredient! Benny was so excited, he ran all the way to Tommy's house. He couldn't wait to tell him.

But just as he knocked on the door, something started to bother Benny. He'd gotten that secret recipe by an accident. He didn't come by it honestly. The door opened and Tommy called him on in. The other boys were in the kitchen, still experimenting with new ingredients for their snow cones.

"Did you ask her?" Tommy asked.

Benny nodded.

"Well, what'd she say?" asked John.

"She said it was a secret," Benny told his friends.

The moral of the story: True character is often revealed when no one is looking.

Note to parents: This story is about the need to do the right thing always. Our founders put barriers in place to help manage man's lesser instincts. There are separation of powers, limits on government authority and personal action, and punishments that fit the crime. They also gave us certain unalienable rights and liberties to protect us from excessive power. But the key to a healthy nation is in the good character of its people.

Questions for Kids

1. What is the first responsibility of our government?

2. What does the government do?

3. How do we get peace?

4. What are taxes and why do we have to pay them?

5. Why do we go to war?

6. Why doesn't everyone get the same things?

7. Is making money bad?

8. Can the government do anything it wants?

9. What do you have when you don't have Capitalism?

10. Why don't some people like Walmart?

11. What is fiscal responsibility?

13. Where does government get its power?

14. Where does government get its power to make people do things?

15. How and why did our country get so much debt?

Part Three

The Origins and Foundations of Liberalism/Progressivism

Part Three Kids' Page

"Don't worry about earning your own way or providing for your own needs. The Liberals in government will find a way to blame our shortcomings on big business or the rich. Once we are proclaimed 'victims,' they will help us."

<u>Mom's and Dad's Mission:</u>

Relate the history and foundations of Liberalism or,
as some call it, Progressivism.

Kids' Page Summary

Our twenty-sixth president, Teddy Roosevelt, was generally Conservative in his tendencies (strong on defense, tough on crime, and skeptical of Congress), but he introduced the progressive income tax wherein the rich not only pay more money in taxes, but they also pay a higher rate. His activist approach to the presidency and his progressive taxation, perhaps inadvertently, paved the way for what Charles Kesler, a senior fellow of the Claremont Institute, professor of government at Claremont McKenna College, and editor of the *Claremont Review of Books*, called the four cycles or waves of Liberalism. Woodrow Wilson, our twenty-eighth president, in the first cycle of Liberalism (political activism), tried to change our Constitution not by constitutional amendment, but by executive leadership and presidential activism. In the second cycle of Liberalism (economic activism), our thirty-second and only three-term president, Franklin D. Roosevelt, used the crisis of the Great Depression to add many government-assistance programs such as Social Security and the Tennessee Valley Authority to our overcommitted coffers. He thought it was government's job to do for the people whatever they could not or would not do for themselves. Although our thirty-sixth president, Lyndon B. Johnson, made great progress with his support for civil rights, in the third cycle of Liberalism (cultural activism), he added the new "rights" of Medicare and Medicaid to our undue burden. He also made his mark by introducing "identity politics" to our country. This meant that who you were and what group you belonged to might in and of itself define you as a victim and qualify you for

government relief. The fourth cycle of Liberalism (big government activism) has come upon us in the current administration,
which is expanding government as never before. Federal
increases in spending, regulations, taxes, and nationaliza-
tion of major private businesses are all designed to promote
social justice as defined by Progressives. These government
programs typically have noble objectives (e.g., universal
health care, environmental protection, and helping the poor);
however, the government's historical success rate at running
such programs is very near zero. Noble the objectives might
be, but the means to achieve these objectives have generally
been flawed. In other words, Liberals often try to do the right
thing with government programs, but too often the programs
just do not work as intended.

The Origins and Foundations of Liberalism/Progressivism

T his seems like a good time in the book to look at what is at the opposite end of the political spectrum Conservatism. Often, taking a good look at the arguments and debating points of an opposing position casts greater light on both those who oppose and those who support a particular proposition. This section attempts to examine why the people of America who do not support Conservatism hold this view.

Why would someone choose against individual freedom, self-reliance, and personal accountability? Why are some against free trade or against the interests of so many free-enterprise businesses that are operating within our laws? How is it that some feel comfortable with the concept of unilateral disarmament or a weakened national defense? Who thinks being soft on crime will eventually reduce crime and aid society? Why do some people appear to feel more empathy for the perpetrators of crimes than for the victims of crimes? Who are these people, and why do they think this way?

First, is it Liberalism or is it Progressivism? They are the same. The term Liberal was hijacked from our founders; they used it to mean support of liberty. After Liberalism was exposed for its true intentions (state or elitist rule), the term Progressivism was invented to take its place.

Progressivism, under any name, seeks to disconnect us from the principles of our founders and to detach us from our history. Progressives believe that the Constitution does not reflect perpetual and undeniable truths; they believe that our founders created the Constitution as a self-serving document to protect their economic interests.

Progressives seek to move beyond the Constitution in part because it uses guaranteed individual liberties to put limits on federal government authority. Progressivism is not to be confused with progress, unless you believe it is progress to be ruled by the elite at the cost of individual liberties, and to abandon the rule of law in favor of the rule of men.

Progressives do not believe it is right that the political principles of our founding fathers should stand in their way to perfect life and government. They believe that the proper role of government is to use its power to control its citizens to establish that which they perceive as fairness and social justice.

To accomplish this they need to destroy the institutional balance of powers put in place by the Constitution because they need centralized power to enforce their elitist view of perfection. They need to eliminate the boundaries that individual rights and liberties impose between the government and its citizens.

Conservatives believe that man can be good but that man cannot be perfected. Therefore, institutional safeguards need to be in place to protect everyday people against man's lesser instincts.

The two enemies of the people are criminals and government, so let us tie the second down with the chains of the constitution so the second will not become the legalized version of the first.

—Often attributed to Thomas Jefferson

Many people describe themselves as Progressives, but what are they "progressing" away from and what is it that they are "progressing" toward? Their isolationist or pacifist tendencies define a substantial group of Progressives. This antiwar group of Liberals seems to feel that if we just mind our own business, rogue nations or terrorists without ties to a particular nation will leave us alone, therefore allowing peace and prosperity to prevail. They see Conservatives as warmongers too ready to engage their perceived enemy in a bloody battle of wills, and they never see Conservatives as liberators of oppressed people or protectors of our nation. Many Liberals do not think of themselves as Socialists (where the government actually owns the means of production), but their tendencies are clearly in the big government Socialist (nanny state) tradition. There are even a few Liberals who admit to being committed Communists.

Most of the voting public who have come down on the side of Liberalism are very likely intelligent and compassionate. They honestly believe that their self-appointed representation of the weak and helpless justifies their mission to multiply the government as the solution to a wide range of existing problems and missed opportunities. Liberals profess to be for the poor and the needy but have increasingly become supporters of the upper-middle-class professional elite, which is top-heavy with journalists, lawyers, and academics. Conservatives disagree with them, but Conservatives recognize that many Liberals are fine and good people.

In trying to understand why some would think this way, we need to examine what Liberalism or Progressivism means to the average Liberal. What principles best describe a Progressive philosophy, what practices best describe a Liberal economic system, and what is the true nature of a Liberal political system? Who started Liberalism? When and why did Liberalism start? And finally, what is Liberalism's ultimate objective?

❧

Chapter 12

A Brief Reminder of the Principles of Conservatism

It is important to focus on the differences to contrast Liberalism with Conservatism. The Conservative view of human nature in part reflects that individuals will naturally pursue self-interest and will take pride in individual accomplishment, which will proliferate into relishing the fruits of a well-lived life of self-reliance. Conservatives embrace personal responsibility and accountability for their own circumstances as well as those of their families and their communities.

Conservatives believe that individuals can fend for and take care of themselves when they are given equal opportunity, equal justice, freedom from the tyranny of an overreaching government, domestic tranquility, and freedom to choose their own path to prosperity and happiness. Conservatives believe that these elements of human nature are natural, right, permanent, and unchanging throughout the generations. Conservatives believe in people.

Conservatives also believe that Free-Market Capitalism provides the structure and the engine that allows millions of people to express their individual creativity, ingenuity, and drive to improve not only the life of the individual, but also to improve the lives of our society as a whole. Conservatives believe that no political or economic system other than Capitalism has ever raised so many individuals out of poverty and despair.

✆

Chapter 13

What Is Liberal or Progressive Philosophy?

How is Liberalism different? Liberals view human nature far differently from Conservatives. Liberals believe that individuals have the natural tendency to pursue their own self-interest but, unlike Conservatives, do not necessarily see this motivation as a wholesome and caring one. Conservatives attempt to harness this natural tendency through a system of laws and the economic structure of Capitalism. Liberals give the impression that this natural inclination of man to pursue self-interest must be changed to serve the greater good of society as a whole. Liberals feel that this pursuit of self-interest too often devolves into excessive greed, manipulation, exploitation of the poor, or even violence.

It also looks as though Liberals view average individuals as incapable of providing for themselves without the substantial help of the government elite. In other words, they appear to see rugged individualism and pursuit of self-interest as impediments to society.

Liberals appear perfectly willing to diminish some of our country's original rights as long as these freedoms are diminished in the name of helping those Liberals perceive as the weaker among us.

Their tendency is often to demonize the successful to justify higher taxes on them to fund Liberal causes. In other words, they are more than ready to hurt one group of individuals to help a more favored group whom they perceive to be in need. Liberals believe that extensive Socialist-like government support not only is the compassionate way to run a country, but also that it works, in spite of its continued failure in the United States and around the world.

The death-knell of the republic had rung as soon as the active power became lodged in the hands of those who sought, not to do justice to all citizens, rich and poor alike, but to stand for one special class and for its interests as opposed the interests of others. —*Teddy Roosevelt, Labor Day speech in Syracuse, NY, September 7, 1903*

It often appears that Liberals are satisfied using flawed means as long as they can say they are chasing noble goals. They seem to feel good if they can say, "We tried to do the right thing," or "We had good intentions," or "We took action on the matter," even if what they tried resulted in abject failure that took them further from their stated objectives.

Take a look at some of the major Liberal causes, such as the War on Poverty, that have not reduced poverty or dependence on government since the programs designed to do just that were introduced more than forty years ago. Look at many of the Liberal programs that overpromised, overspent, and underdelivered that have had little impact on problems they were supposed to solve. Consider the government initiative called "Healthy Start," designed primarily to reduce by 50 percent the rate of infant mortality in poor communities. When the government-sponsored research on the efficacy of this program did not produce the expected results, the results of the research were abandoned. The Liberal solution is and has been (and probably will continue to be) to go on with the program and expand it by throwing more money at it. Liberals have, in effect, become professional advocates who want to use the government and other people's money to correct all manner of social ills as they perceive and define them. Plus, if along the way to "helping" those whom they view as society's victims, Liberals can find a way to demonize and punish the hospital companies, the pharmaceutical industry, or the doctors who trained for twelve years for the job, all the better.

Conservatives would not abandon people who are in dire circumstances. They agree that the poor and infirm need help and that helping them is a proper and just responsibility of society. The Conservative solution would be to prioritize this program along with all others, to look at available resources (public and private), to measure the effectiveness of the services provided, and to determine how to deal with the issue. Conservatives believe that good intentions and noble goals are only the beginning, not the end. They would not continue a program that did not work just so they could say they are "doing something about the matter" to an important constituency. If the objectives of the program were valid and deemed to be a priority, Conservatives would look to change the program so it had a better chance to achieve its original objectives.

Liberals feel that there are a huge number of problems and opportunities that are so big or so important that only the government, and specifically the elitists and bureaucrats who run the government, can solve them. Liberals feel the need to criticize success and achievement as if all individual or business prosperity were achieved on the backs of the poor and the helpless. Liberals often use populist and righteous-sounding rhetoric (e.g., fairness and social justice) to describe their utopian goals of helping people achieve their promises of a near-perfect society. It would be better if they just found a way that worked to help these people.

℘

Chapter 14

When and Why
Did Liberalism Start?

(Some Teddy Roosevelt
and a lot of Woodrow Wilson)

T he first real rumblings of Liberalism began in 1901 when
Teddy Roosevelt assumed office after the assassination of
President William McKinley. Teddy Roosevelt, a Republican, took actions that were consistent with both Conservatism
and Liberalism. On the Conservative side, he was strong on
defense ("Speak softly and carry a big stick"), he was skeptical
of Congress, and he was tough on what he considered to be
crime and corruption in unions, political machines, and antitrust
activities of monopolies. However, on the Liberal side, Roosevelt
championed the idea of a progressive income tax (a graduated
tax wherein the rich would not only pay more money in taxes,
but also at a higher rate), and he believed in an activist presidency. The White House Web site's bio on him (www.whitehouse
.gov/about/presidents/TheodoreRoosevelt) states, "He took the
view that the President as a 'steward of the people' should take

whatever action necessary for the public good unless expressly forbidden by law or the Constitution. 'I did not usurp power,' he wrote, 'but I did greatly broaden the use of executive power.'" In addition, Roosevelt also expanded the area dedicated to what we now call National Forests. Although Teddy Roosevelt supported a concept he called Progressivism (his use of the term referred to the expanded use of science, technology, and engineering), he was clearly an activist president with significant progressive initiatives, but he was not a classic Liberal and certainly not a Socialist. Here is a quote that might provide some insight to Teddy Roosevelt's perception of those in the legislative branch:

When they call the roll in the Senate, the Senators do not know whether to answer "Present" or "Not Guilty."

—Teddy Roosevelt

Liberalism, under different names, began a little more than a hundred years ago with Theodore Roosevelt's progressive taxation and activist presidency (he might have inadvertently provided the funding Liberals would use, but he did not embrace the entire Liberal philosophy). As described very effectively by Professor Charles Kesler, Liberalism really found its footing with the first questioning on the adequacy of the Constitution as the law of the land by Woodrow Wilson, our twenty-eighth president, elected as a Democrat in 1912. Wilson came to believe that the Constitution was an eighteenth-century document that required substantial modification to meet twentieth-century needs. Wilson was not the first president to expand executive powers; however, he was the first president to express major criticisms of the Constitution. He, along with our thirty-second president, Franklin D. Roosevelt, believed that the Constitution could more easily be changed through activist reinterpretation and presidential leadership than through formal and legal amendment. Woodrow Wilson was also the first who considered leading the country to accept this constitutional reinterpretation was part of the president's job. Both Wilson and FDR knew the American people would not stand for legislative language that smacked of Socialism, and they knew that the people would not approve of amending the Constitution to include the radical changes they supported. So they came up with rhetoric that included new terms such as *progressivism* and *a living constitution.*

Although Wilson was not the first president who openly believed that a constitutional amendment was not necessary to change the law of the land, to expand executive powers, or to implement his personal vision of the future, previous presidents limited presidential activism to such issues as use of force, wartime authority, and foreign policy. Wilson focused on selling the public on the idea that severe and urgent problems existed and that he had the answers. He more fully developed the political concept of using a crisis to gain political advantage. Once he convinced the public that urgent fixes were needed, he could just assume the new powers without the tedious legal battle of congressional approval or a constitutional amendment. He realized that once he had public opinion on his side, many opposing politicians who might otherwise have put up roadblocks to his intended actions would just go along to get along. With the exception of expanding executive authority during times of war, most of our presidents prior to (and a few after) Wilson believed it was their responsibility to run the office of the president as the founders of our country prescribed the presidential authorities and responsibilities in the Constitution. To paraphrase Charles Kesler, Wilson's presidential activism was the first cycle or wave of Liberalism.

∽

Chapter 15

Why Did They Feel the Need to Start Liberalism or Progressivism?

Woodrow Wilson believed that some of the very foundations upon which the Constitution was based were flawed. In particular, it appears he thought the element of human nature related to pursuit of self-interest, which he saw as selfish and egotistical, was wrong. Plus, even if this self-interest were natural, it did not fit into his more Socialistic view of what he saw as good governance. To Liberals, government was not in place just to ensure an equal opportunity of all in a safe and protected way. It was there to help ensure that increasing numbers of people achieved outcomes that Liberals perceived as more equitable. That is, Wilson believed that equal opportunity was not enough; it was the government's role to level not only the playing field, but also the score. Conservatives believed that free and safe individuals could and would ensure a prosperous and free destiny while Liberals believed that most individuals required more than just freedom, opportunity, and safety; they required government assistance.

ॐ

Chapter 16

The Economic and Political System of Liberalism

T
o achieve the Liberal view of destiny, government needed to be expanded. New social and economic "rights" needed to be established and guaranteed by the government. FDR became the greatest champion of Liberalism and used the crisis of the Great Depression of the 1930s to help him reach his goals. FDR furthered this movement by attempting to merge these new "social rights" with the original rights the founders envisioned and detailed in the Constitution.

FDR was very clever at "passing" these new rights. He sold them not as new rights, but as a "continuation" of old rights. He emphasized that Americans had the same rights but now just had more of them. This merger of rights, however, did not occur without conflict.

With new rights came new duties. Someone had to pay for these new rights and "entitlements." Since the government did not then, and does not now, actually earn any money, it had to get whatever additional funds it needed from the people. In other words, the government had to raise taxes to pay for its new programs. This might be where Liberals developed the concept of using other people's money (OPM) to fund their social justice, social engineering, and vote-buying initiatives. There was a saying at the time: *"Don't tax me; don't tax thee; tax that man behind the tree."*

If Congress can do whatever in their discretion
can be done by money, and will promote the General Welfare,
the government is no longer a limited one possessing enumerated
powers, but an indefinite one subject to particular exceptions.

—James Madison

FDR became a master at using the crisis of the Great Depression to institute new entitlement programs. Plus, he could get votes to support his welfare plans for the many by promising to pay for them

It is easy to be generous with other peoples' money.

by taxing only the few. He made it appear that the money required to fund his new rights and programs would come from only such sources as big business and rich people, people who many Liberals maintained probably did not get their money through hard work anyway. He made businesses and rich people "those men behind the tree."

∽

Chapter 17

Liberalism as a Government System—FDR's New Deal

W here Wilson expanded executive authority to help facilitate his Liberal vision for America, FDR developed the concept of a "living constitution" that could be reinterpreted to achieve his needs. He and his Liberal legislators focused their efforts on recruiting justices who believed in this philosophy of reinterpretation. These jurists became what we now call "activist judges."

Liberals found a new tool, the court system, to right that which they believed to be wrong in the Constitution but could not change through constitutional means. Conservatives believed that many of the items that FDR called new social and economic rights (e.g., right to a job, right to health care, and right to a retirement fund) were good things, but they believed as the founders did and did not consider them to be fundamental, unalienable human rights.

Conservatives were concerned that these newly proposed social and economic rights would come with new and unaffordable duties. They could also see that certain existing constitutionally guaranteed individual freedoms would likely be lost or diminished as these new burdensome obligations were taken on. Conservatives realized from history that as government collectivism grows, individual freedoms diminished. Liberalism came in through the back door by leveraging the crisis of the depression, the use of clever rhetoric, and the newfound activist judges to modify the Constitution without amendment or the people's or states' approval.

FDR, like others who followed him, realized that the best time to sell his radical agenda of new social and economic rights was during a crisis. The Great Depression, which lasted throughout the 1930s, gave him just such an opportunity, and the deep economic recession of today has offered Liberals a similar opportunity to cast their radical changes in government and society not as sweeping revisions to the Constitution, but just as "common sense solutions" to current problems.

New Deal; Right to a Job and a Vacation
with Other Peoples' Money

FDR's New Deal further promoted the concept that individuals could not be counted on to provide for their own social needs and benefits; therefore, the government had to do it for them. Until Wilson and FDR, it took the virtues of hard work, ingenuity, and commitment to sacrifice for family needs to subsist and prosper. However, with every new government-assistance program, there came some diminishing of personal responsibility. The more the government provided subsidy, the less the individual had to provide for himself. More than six decades later, we now have a vicious and heartless cycle of government dependency that has lasted through generations of families. The very people that big government attempted to help have suffered greatly from this "help." These people needed temporary financial help, but they also needed permanent incentives and opportunities to become self-sufficient. Here again, we see a Liberal initiative with good intentions that just did not work as intended. Charles Kesler described FDR's economic activism as the second wave of Liberalism.

ତ୍ତ

Chapter 18

Freedom from a Culture of Personal Responsibility— LBJ's "Great Society"

Lyndon Baines Johnson brought about the "Great Society," which Charles Kesler called the third wave of twentieth-century Liberalism in the 1960s. LBJ made great strides in promoting and implementing needed civil rights legislation. However, the cultural Great Society, in addition to bringing about important civil rights, took our nation down the road of more government dependency and less personal responsibility, all in the name of compassion and fairness.

This cycle of Liberalism emphasized cultural and, at times, countercultural factors. It brought New Deal–style government rights and entitlements coupled with the reinterpretations and the concept of a living constitution to form a new type of freedom. After FDR's government-assistance policies and programs, under LBJ came the beginnings of government's responsibilities for providing individuals with their survival necessities. This government-assistance effort relieved many in our country of the personal responsibility for attaining the level of capability to obtain these items. LBJ's new cultural rights helped many people incapable of helping themselves, but it also allowed a large segment of capable people in the United States to live a new kind of freedom, a freedom from the old-fashioned virtue of daily hard work.

This transformation of character and pride was all done to support the Liberal vision of destiny as seen through the filter of the Great Society. It was liberation from the virtuous life of hard work, providing for one's family, and making sacrifices to improve the chances of success for one's children.

LBJ and the Liberal movement realized to ensure these new rights, a great price would need to be paid. In Liberal tradition, he moved once again to tax the few to pay for the many. Social

The Great Society: A New Freedom, "Victimology,"
the Freedom from Personal Responsibility

engineering has not only been ineffective, but also never cheap. The price and efficacy of these new rights, however, were of no issue to the beneficiaries, primarily because they were paid for with other people's money. This cultural liberation gave new energy to the concept of *identity politics,* where individuals gained rights and privileges primarily because of the nature of the group to which they belonged. Under LBJ, the government could gain large groups of voters (voting blocs) by acknowledging real or perceived wrongs and offering to give advantages, subsidies, or reparations to these groups who were described as victims of American society.

These tactics show the political genius of certain brands of Liberalism. The focus on specific voting blocs greatly helped to further the Liberal agenda and to develop the notion that Liberals were fighting for the underdog. The institution of identity politics helped LBJ and others turn privileges into rights, and once there were rights, broad categories of citizens who claimed repression could be given aid and advantage in many forms. With the passing of certain responsibilities from individuals to the government, Liberals felt they could successfully argue that their government assistance initiatives were making society greater. It was commonly said at the time that with the "helping hand" of government, *the future will be better than the present and the present is better than the past.*

The cultural revolution of the 1960s freed everyone to pursue his or her passion without reason and without personal responsibility. Theodore Roosevelt's presidential activism and progressive taxation found new government funding that many Liberals felt needed to be spent. Woodrow Wilson's constitutional activism (the first cycle of Liberalism) created new executive authorities to make changes in government that were developed out of thin air. FDR's New Deal (the second cycle of Liberalism) made government assistance a right for certain categories of individuals whom

FDR felt could not be counted on to provide their own housing, jobs, or education. And because of LBJ's Great Society (the third cycle of Liberalism), individuals gained additional rights and advantages just because of who they were and with what group they were identified.

As a side note, I give much credit to Professor Charles Kesler for his description of what I call the Liberal cycles. However, many of the above comments did not come from Kesler and I do not profess to represent his views.

Chapter 19

How Do Liberals Defend Liberalism?

It does not take long after turning on the TV, listening to the radio, opening a newspaper or magazine, conversing at dinner parties, or going online to find the many defenses of Liberalism. Some are subtle and some are very harsh and direct. Most are filled with emotion, well-constructed (often carefully parsed) rhetoric, and regularly repeated talking points that seem to come from an anti-Conservative central planning committee. I admit I have no idea whether such a "committee" actually exists.

Again, it seems that many of these supporters and defenders of Liberalism are good people preaching what they believe. Following are responses to many of these Liberal comments and accusations. I have culled these Liberal questions and comments from many sources.

Chapter 20

Conservative Defenses against Liberal Accusations

L et me start by agreeing to disagree on certain common Liberal accusations such as "Bush lied about WMDs in Iraq" and "Reagan didn't end the Cold War." I don't know if President George W. Bush lied about weapons of mass destruction, but I don't think so. It appeared to me that nearly the whole world, including the intelligence agencies of many other countries, high-ranking Liberals in Congress, and many Liberal news outlets such as the *New York Times* all believed that WMDs likely existed in Iraq. I felt the war could have been managed much better, but I think Bush was being honest in his stated concerns about the tyranny, oppression, and tangible threats related to Saddam Hussein.

As to Reagan and the end of the Cold War, there were likely many factors related to the timing of the fall of the Berlin Wall and the demise of the Soviet Union. The Soviet Union appeared to be crumbling under the repression of Communism, and there is no doubt about the many failures, economic and otherwise, of Communist central planning. However, recognizing that my position on these accusations might be viewed as just more Conservative bias, I believe that Ronald Reagan's tough talk regarding the Soviet Union's evil ways and, in particular, huge weapons buildup that the Soviets could not match were significant factors in the fall of the Soviet Empire.

There is a group of common Liberal accusations that fall into the category of confusing (perhaps purposely) Conservatives with Republicans. Many Republicans have strayed from their Conservative roots (e.g., George W. Bush dramatically increased government entitlements when he signed the Prescription Drugs for Seniors law), and it is obvious to the most casual observer that some Republicans never had Conservative roots (in fact, this is so common that there is a name for them: RINOs, or Republicans In Name Only).

The questions of why George W. Bush (GWB) ran up such large deficits and often seemed to lack fiscal discipline are valid questions. But the answers to these questions have at least two parts: First, the costs of 9/11 terrorism, Hurricane Katrina, and the wars in Iraq and Afghanistan dramatically increased federal deficits. I feel these aspects of spending above plan were mostly unavoidable, although Liberals could and will argue about government inefficiencies and the need for the wars. Second, GWB also vetoed very few spending bills. Republicans in Congress helped the passage of many unnecessary spending bills, and GWB himself expanded Liberal programs such as prescription drugs for seniors.

When a Republican takes Liberal actions, he or she is, at least in part, a Liberal. The fact that Liberal programs were supported by Republicans means only that many Republicans have occasional Liberal tendencies and that many appear to be checking surveys and polls just like many Liberals.

Note: *The huge and at least partially indefensible deficits run up by GWB pale when compared to those created in the first year of our current administration.*

There are a number of other accusations and criticisms of Conservatives commonly offered by Liberals:

- Why is it fair that under Capitalism some individuals make $10 per hour while others make ten, twenty, or thirty times more?
- Why are Conservatives against unrestricted abortion?
- Why do Conservatives support bans on certain illegal drugs?
- Why don't Conservatives support women and minorities?
- Why are Conservatives against environmental regulations?
- Why did Conservatives oppose much of FDR's New Deal?
- Why don't Conservatives support special rights for gays and lesbians?
- Why do Conservatives support only traditional marriage between a man and a woman?
- Why don't Conservatives support more civil rights such as habeas corpus, Miranda rights, or the right to an attorney for foreign terrorists or those captured on the battlefield?
- Why don't Conservatives admit to their racial bias, homophobic tendencies, and insensitivity to the poor, all of which have been exposed by the actions of the vast right-wing conspiracy?

The questions above represent only some of the many common talking-point questions that are often raised by Liberals. My answers are as follows:

- Conservatives believe that our Constitution provides for equal opportunities, not equal outcomes. This question implies that because there are wage inequities, Capitalism might be inherently unfair and, therefore, insensitive to those most in need. By no means is this the case. First, the question that needs to be asked is not whether Capitalism in inherently unfair, but whether Capitalism differs from other alternatives in fairness or in sensitivity to those in need. In other words, is Socialism, Communism, or Fascism fairer than Capitalism? Few would say so. Under Capitalism, society puts a price on all labor, services, and products generally based on supply and demand. Therefore, wages are established by the aggregate actions of our citizenry, and there is no evidence whatsoever that wages and rewards established by government central planners are more equitable than those set by Capitalism. Second, as to fairness and caring for the needy, Capitalism has raised more people out of poverty and despair than all other forms of government combined. There is no argument in this response that Capitalism is perfect or that it cannot be improved in any way. Indeed, perfection in any human system is an unattainable goal; the best we can strive for is continuous improvements.

- Conservatives support bans on unrestricted abortions because they believe that at some point during pregnancy (and there is a range of beliefs on the exact point, even among Conservatives) there is another life besides the mother's that also deserves protection. And Conservatives are for protecting innocent life.

- Actually, there are serious arguments for legalizing certain currently illegal drugs that have come from notable Conservatives (e.g., Bill Buckley) as well as many Liberals. However, I take my queue from law enforcement and hospital officials who do not view the use of illegal drugs as benign or victimless. In too many cases, minor drug use turns into to major drug use. In addition, the addictive nature of most illegal drugs too often results in criminal behavior (beyond banned drug use) and in destroyed families.

- Conservatives actually support both women and minorities. The primary Liberal argument that Conservatives are against women's rights is related to the Conservative opposition to unrestricted abortions. The "fetuses' rights versus women's rights" issue was addressed above; Conservatives' support for innocent life in no way reflects a lack of support for women. Liberals contend that Conservatives do not believe all men are created equal, as evidenced by their perceived bias against minorities, their lack of support for special rights for certain groups of people, their disdain for affirmative- action quotas, and their general opposition to open borders and unlimited immigration. This implication is false. Conservatives believe attempting to resolve past discrimination against one group with future discrimination against another is misguided. They also believe that legal immigrants deserve all the rights reserved for them in the Constitution, but they believe that illegal or unrestricted immigration is wrong and not in the best interests of the nation. These beliefs are not inconsistent with supporting minorities, in spite of the fact that they might be inconsistent with the positions held by some organizations that represent or claim they are representing minority groups.

- Conservatives are against pollution and not against reasonable and cost-effective environmental regulations. The fact that many Conservatives feel that certain environmental regulations have been abused does not make them anti-environment. The fact that most Conservatives would provide water to Northern California to save human life and farming (perhaps at the expense of the delta smelt fish to the north) reflects only the Conservative perspective that saving and protecting human life represents a higher priority to them than saving a fish that might or might not actually be endangered. The fact that many Conservatives believe that Liberal environmental programs such as the Endangered Species Act have been used as disingenuous weapons against reasonable human development does not imply that Conservatives are for unrestricted and unplanned development. Because many Conservatives are in favor of environmentally safe domestic drilling for oil and natural gas does not make them anti-environment; it shows only that they see energy independence as a more important goal than preserving such areas as the small patch of frozen land dubbed the Arctic National Wildlife Refuge in Alaska in its pristine, natural state: frozen. Although Liberals might not think so, Conservatives live on the same planet as everyone else and strongly desire to see it protected.

- It was not that Conservatives thought nothing should be done to help people who were plunged into need by the Great Depression. It was that they felt the Socialistic central planning of FDR's New Deal was the wrong thing to do either because it was inconsistent with constitutional authorities or that much of it just would not provide the durable level of relief needed. Conservatives would have focused on putting America's millions of entrepreneurs to work on the problem and aimed their help more at small businesses and reduced tax burdens for all. FDR's Liberal New Deal relied on adding inefficient and often ineffective permanent government assistance programs that were sold as temporary fixes to transient problems. Many of these still burden us today.

- Conservatives believe that gays and lesbians should retain all the rights of other citizens. Conservatives are against discrimination and are for tolerance. However, many Conservatives believe that the lifestyles presented by these groups are inconsistent with their own personal values and do not want schools or other government organizations undermining their personal value system in requiring teaching the equal validity of untraditional families in traditional family structures.

- Conservatives support what is known as traditional marriage for many reasons. The privilege to marry is a traditional privilege that allows one person to marry another of the opposite gender. All people, including gays and lesbians, have this privilege. Marriage is not a privilege that relates to all unions (e.g., marriage to multiple partners or marriage to someone of the same genders). One reason is that Conservatives believe that society gains much from cultural values that have survived the tests of time. They further believe that much has been lost over the past forty years or so by the abandonment of many cultural values (note in this response I am referring to time-tested traditions of civilization, not just religious traditions). It has been reported in many serious publications that as many as 40 percent of all births are out of wedlock and that half of all teens will have used an illegal drug before they finish high school. Most Conservatives place their belief that marriage needs to be between only a man and woman with many of these other cultural values that keep society strong.

- As to rights for terrorists, Conservatives believe that when a foreign national is caught committing an act of terrorism or is captured fighting against us on a battlefield, that individual requires only detention and military justice. Holding this position is not at all inconsistent with supporting civil rights for American citizens.

- As with the majority of Americans, Conservatives believe in tolerance and equal rights for all people irrespective of race, color, creed, or sexual orientation. What Conservatives are against is special rights for some categories of people that do not apply to all people. When Conservatives disagree with proposed Liberal solutions, they are often criticized as opposing or being insensitive to the people for whom these solutions were intended. As to the vast right-wing conspiracy, I wish there were one. To the contrary, too many elected Conservatives, with the exception of the Reagan era, have been reticent to respond to Liberal criticisms and too quiet in expressing their own views.

I believe that at times it is difficult for some Conservatives to effectively respond to the emotional and often populist rhetoric advanced by Liberals. Many of these carefully composed talking points sound at first blush like reasonable and compelling arguments, whether or not their false premises beget their conclusions or the logical structures of their arguments are invalid. "Bush lied" makes for a good sound bite and fits nicely on a bumper sticker whether the statement is supported or refuted by the facts. Using the mistakes of misguided Republicans to condemn Conservative philosophy also makes for good sound bites, although it is well known that many Republicans are not Conservative and that the staunchest of Conservative Republicans occasionally go off point.

Recently a Liberal friend asked me why, if Conservatives were for freedom and liberty, they didn't support the Revolutionary War. This was another perhaps inadvertent attempt to confuse the facts with semantics rather than relying on truth and logic. The "Conservatives" she was referring to were *British* Conservatives (otherwise known as Tories). These Conservatives of the time were completely unconnected to modern-day Conservatives. They were in favor of conserving allegiance to the British. The historic Conservatives related to modern-day Conservatives were not the Tories; they were the founders of our country who declared independence from Great Britain and fought in the Revolutionary War for America's freedom.

The question of whether or not the Liberals' big-government fixes sound compelling is not really the right issue. What one needs to ask is do these big-government programs work better than free-market solutions, are they priorities, and can we afford them? I would offer that the history of their failure is nearly absolute. Conservatives believe there is a purpose for government (a limited purpose), but their real faith is in the power of individual people. I hope the responses provided above and the following analysis proves helpful in debunking the many false accusations against Conservatives.

∞

Chapter 21

The Truly Needy, the Noble, and the Ignoble

M any objective onlookers see three classes of Liberals: the truly needy, the noble, and the ignoble.

The truly needy support many Conservative and Liberal programs to help them brave the circumstances in which they exist. The poor, the disabled, and the victims of terrorism or natural disaster are cared for from both sides of the aisle. However, Liberals have been so successful at public relations that they have convinced many of the truly needy that Conservatives do not perceive or care about their daily battles and pain. Both Liberals and Conservatives recognize that these people require and deserve substantial help from society to help ease their pain and to survive their infirmities, but Liberals are better at expressing empathy, and therefore, Liberals often seem to care more.

A reasonable perception of the *noble and idealist people,* who are truly altruistic, is that they often believe the good intentions of Liberals deserve their support, regardless of the lack of results achieved or negative consequences derived. These believers appear to think that all of the elected officials—especially those who are Liberal—in Washington, D.C., are angels. They are not. They often perceive Conservatives as supporters of only the rich and of big business. They have the sense that big business conspires to take advantage of those in need and that the rich gained their riches through means other than honest efforts, ingenuity, and hard work. These people love employees but have great disdain for employers. They are fans of the fruits of investment but have a harsh view of investors. Somehow they cannot see the connections. They often feel more than they reason. They do not see the harm in long-term government dependency, and they feel their support of Liberals is truly noble. Plus, they do not consider the fact that modern-day Conservative principles were first articulated by our founders.

There are those who fly the Liberal flag for personal gain. In many circles, these Liberals are known as *ignoble*. This harsh language is used to describe the many elected officials from both

No matter how noble the words or programs or policies, Liberalism simply does not help the people intended to be helped.

sides of the aisle who support Liberal initiatives, in large part, to buy votes. These are unprincipled people who spend their time advancing class warfare and reading polls to find out what they need to support. These people hide under the philosophy of Liberalism and support nearly every spending program because they believe these tactics will get them elected or reelected. Their true goal is to acquire more power, prestige, and wealth for themselves. They proudly support such unsavory and undemocratic programs as earmarks. They push through legislation that is designed to help themselves, their friends, and their campaign contributors. It is easy for this group to vote for legislation they have not read because they have the results of political polls to support them.

Chapter 22

What Are the Ultimate Objectives of Liberalism?

The genius of Liberalism is they often have *no obvious final objective*. They profess to seek a utopian world that they are unable to adequately describe. They seem to believe that there is no end to the "reform" to be done or the "progress" to be achieved. There is always more "fairness" to be realized and "righteous" work to be done. They never run out of important causes because they know how to invent new ones if the old ones tarnish. Their social justice and social engineering will never be finished.

Liberals can always justify more and more government growth, irrespective of limited resources, under the guise of helping the little people or the helpless. This group appears to believe that the Liberal elite are so superior to the average person that only they can be trusted as the nation's policymakers. Only they can perceive the crisis around the corner, and only they can help people avoid it. Oddly, Liberals who appear to believe they are our intellectual superiors hate to be called "elites." Perhaps that is because they are not truly elites who have excelled in some particular field of expertise or achieved some great accomplishment. Mostly they are just politicians or pundits with opinions that they tout as exceptional. They think it is their job to run the country, when it is their job to merely give their opinion, report the news, or represent the people. They think it is their responsibility to protect the helpless (which, of course, sounds noble). However, they view us all as helpless. We are not.

So what do Liberals really want? If you ask Liberals what the world would look like if they could wave a magic wand and achieve all their goals, they will not give a valid answer. Would they be satisfied if the government took all the money from individuals, owned all the private companies, controlled every product we buy, and spent 100 percent of our gross national product and all of our borrowing power on entitlements? They don't know. Do they want the government to control 50 percent of all commerce, and do they want a 100 percent tax on people making more than a million dollars a year? They cannot or will not answer. My suspicion is that

What Do Liberals Really Want?

Liberals Really Want a Bigger "Fair Share"
or More, More, More of Your Money and More and More Power

too many Liberal politicians have their personal circumstances in mind when they vote for legislation. What do they want? I suspect the answer is all too often: as much as they can get.

When will it stop? It is likely Liberal politicians will keep reaching for more and more power and wealth until the diminishing returns cripple the nation. The people of America need to take responsibility for themselves and their government and stop them.

෨෪

Chapter 23

Twenty-first-century Liberalism—Big Government
(The Nanny State)

Currently the Liberal leaders with their clever rhetoric down-play the historical inefficiencies of big government and the known negative consequences of an unimaginably high federal debt. They have used the "financial crisis" and the current economic recession (as FDR did in the 1930s) to pass whopping enti-tlements and pet and pork projects then pretended that their actions are not radical and their philosophies are not Statist or Socialist.

I believe there are more instances of the abridgement of freedom of the people by gradual and silent encroachments of those in power than by violent and sudden usurpations.

—James Madison

As a precursor to Liberalism, Theodore Roosevelt provided the funding vehicle (progressive taxation) that would be used by the

231

politicians who followed him. No doubt the success of his aggressive presidential activism also inspired many current and future Liberals. Woodrow Wilson, in the first cycle of Liberalism, orchestrated a new, expanded role of the presidency to reform our governing documents by establishing the concept of executive interpretation and a "living constitution." FDR, in the second cycle of Liberalism, continued these new executive powers and the new Constitutional reinterpretations that provided new economic rights and put in place a whole new set of government assistance programs to support nearly anyone he perceived was in need of help. The third cycle of Liberalism, which includes the steps taken in the first two cycles, adds the concept of identity politics and cultural group rights established by LBJ to the Liberal programs that already existed. Now the fourth cycle of Liberalism is expanding government to new levels, regulating more and more of America, nationalizing major private businesses, and running up debts that are incomprehensible. Perhaps, as Charles Kesler suggests, this group is trying to complete the Liberal agenda. With an initially popular president, with activist judges at his side, and one-party control of Congress, Liberals are using the living constitution, the bully pulpit, a judiciary that is becoming increasingly activist in its rulings, and legislative majorities in an attempt to bring full Liberal control over as much of our economy and our lives as is possible.

I predict future happiness for Americans
if they can prevent the government from wasting the labors
of the people under the pretense of taking care of them.

—Thomas Jefferson

In today's marketplace we are seeing more and more govern-ment interference, unnecessary regulation, and burdensome control over our everyday lives and businesses. The lessons we have learned from history, experience, reason, conscience, and morality need to be revisited, and it needs to be done right here and right now. The concentration of excessive power in government is a real danger, for the concentration of power has always led to corruption and malfeasance. Jurisdiction and power need to be dispersed to keep it just and under control. It is now common for individuals to be categorized and put into support groups, and once there are support groups, there is the expectation of government support. The longtime Liberal goal of ensuring their reelection by expanding government dependence and creating a huge entitlement state has almost come to fruition. Liberals know that when you rob Peter to pay Paul, you can always count on the support of Paul. The only real question is whether all of this Liberal power, however temporary or permanent, can overcome the will of the people.

Parable #6

"The Easy Way"

There's one other kid on the block we haven't talked about. EZ Rider is what Tommy and his friends call him. You'll see him riding his red-and-yellow tricycle up and down the sidewalk in front of his house, hour after hour.

"I'm Ernest Zelmann, Jr.," he'll be happy to tell you. "I'm four years and eleven months old, and I can write my name in cursive. My mother says I am a little genius. I won a beautiful child contest when I was two." EZ is an only child. He is a little spoiled.

All right, EZ is a *lot* spoiled.

All that summer, you'd find him near one of the lemonade stands, riding his tricycle in and around and among the people gathered there. "I have a dog named Buster, and he cost a lot of money and has won several major prizes. Get me one o' them pink snow cones while you're up there, OK?"

EZ thinks he should get whatever he wants. And if he doesn't get it, he gets mad. "You want me to start crying really loud and hold my breath till my mother runs out here to see what's wrong with poor baby Ernest?" EZ usually gets what he wants.

"Hey, EZ Rider, here's a nickel. Go buy a cookie over at the boys' stand," Rosie would say just to get rid of him.

"Hey, EZ Rider, here's a quarter. Go buy somethin' at the girls' stand," Tommy would say.

EZ liked it when people gave him things. EZ *expected* people to give him things.

It was mid-August when EZ wheeled up to the boys' stand on his tricycle and said, "This Saturday is my birthday party, and you can all come. It will be a circus theme, and there will be a blow-up bouncer in my front yard. We will have a clown and ice cream. Come by the house later, and I'll give you a list of things you can get me."

Tommy and his friends weren't quite sure what to say. "Sorry, EZ," Tommy said at last. "But, um, er, ah, Saturday's our busiest day. I don't think I can make it."

"Me neither. Sorry," said John, Benny, Roger, and Robbie. "Gotta work. Lotta work that day. Bummer, huh?"

EZ just shrugged and pedaled over to the girls' stand. "My five-year-old birthday party is this Saturday, and it will be a circus theme, and I will tell you what I want you give me."

But the girls had the same answer for him. "We have to work at the stand. Sorry, EZ. Maybe next year?"

EZ just shrugged and headed home.

There was a circus-themed blow-up bouncer in his front yard on Saturday. Ernest's two cousins and some friends from his dad's work showed up. Other than that, it was a small party. It was very small and very quiet. Even the clown didn't look too happy.

Later, when it was over and the inflatable bouncer was being hauled away, EZ Rider rode his tricycle over to the girls' pink lemonade stand. It was the hottest part of the afternoon, and there were big crowds at both of the stands. EZ rode in and around and among the people waiting in line.

"I'm Ernest Zelmann, Jr.," he told anybody who would listen. "I'm five years old, and one time I won a beautiful child contest. Get me one o' them snow cones, OK?"

The moral of the story: The world owes no one anything, and you shouldn't expect an easy ride from this country.

Note to parents: This story is about our nation's guarantee of "life, liberty, and the pursuit of happiness." It tells of the disappointing reality of always being dependent on others and waiting for someone else to take care of you. There is no lasting satisfaction in being a burden to others. The same is true with our nation. There are people who require assistance, and we, as a society, give them that help. But the greatest gift is self-reliance.

Questions for Kids

1. What are Progressives progressing away from or toward?

2. Shouldn't the government help the poor?

3. What is wrong with Liberalism? It sounds nice.

4. Where did Liberalism come from, and who started it?

5. What is vote-buying?

6. What do you mean by "other people's money"?

7. What do Liberals want?

8. Why is big government bad?

9. Why is the media biased toward Liberals?

The Practical Applications of Conservative Principles to Current Issues

Part Four Kids' Page

"Will the government start buying lemonade stands if they don't make money? Is man really making the planet hotter, or are we just no longer in an Ice Age?"

Mom's and Dad's Mission:

Relate how to apply Conservative principles to everyday situations by providing examples of how I have done so.

Kids' Page Summary

Part IV gives examples of how I have applied my own Common Sense Conservative principles to the political issues we face today. Its purpose is to show how to convert theories and principles into everyday decisions. The subjects of illegal immigration or private-industry bailouts are complex and require considerable thought. The issues relating to what many call "man-made global warming," regardless of whether or not we know it truly exists, are important. How does a Common Sense Conservative feel about redistribution of wealth as a priorty of government, and how do we feel about the notion of taking money earned by one person and giving it to another who did not earn it?

What should we do about getting everybody health insurance? Should the old and the young really pay for those who lose their health insurance? Is this an unalienable right? Does not having *health insurance* mean the same as not having *health care?* If we made health insurance available to everyone, would that fix the high cost and make everything all right?

How much should we know about how our laws are made? Is it acceptable for lawmakers to make any law they want and just let us (we the people) learn about it later? Is a judge or a justice supposed to enforce our laws as they were written, or should he rule based on what he personally thinks is right? Why is our education system not working so well, and why wouldn't everyone want to do something about it?

Should we drill for more oil and gas and risk more pollution, or should we just make smaller cars and wait for new technologies? Can we really make our enemies like us by abandoning our friends and using better public relations? Is this right and would these steps make us safer? Can the government really fix the economy, or is it private business that creates prosperity? Who or what caused the housing problems, and what should we do about protecting innocent life? These are real-life questions we need to answer now.

The Practical Applications of Conservative Principles to Current Issues

The following statements reflect how I have applied my own brand of Common Sense Conservative principles, as detailed in the book, to current events and affairs. I have been advised by many to omit this part of the book to avoid putting myself at risk of strong criticism. I acknowledge this potential, but I feel that this section is necessary to help others apply Common Sense Conservative theory and philosophy (as I see it) to the real world.

I do not represent all Conservatives or even all moms. The only Conservative or mom I represent is myself. I understand that some of my positions on certain issues might be controversial and that many will disagree with me, but these are my opinions.

Chapter 24

Illegal Immigration

Close the borders to stop the influx of illegal drugs, weapons, terrorists, and criminals. Develop an immigrant work-permit program that has significant fines and penalties for businesses and individuals hiring people without the permit. This work-permit program would also need to include thorough background checks for those wanting employment here, including those who have already arrived in this country through other-than-legal channels. This might not make it right, but my sense is that most illegal immigrants are good people fulfilling a legitimate workplace need who came here with the tacit approval of the U.S. government and the support of many businesses. Whatever the just and legal solution is to the issue of people working here illegally, respect their dignity and treat them with compassion. However, violent criminals and felons are in a completely different category, and we need to deal with them swiftly and surely. Leave the citizenship issue alone until the borders are secure, the criminals are in jail or deported, and a well-operating work-permit program is in place. Deport all illegal immigrants who have already been convicted of felonies, and do not let them back in the country. Does it matter that if we adopted the current immigration laws of Mexico, we would be called racists?

Chapter 25

Bailouts

L et the Capitalist system work. Let good companies succeed and prosper, and let the bad companies fail and get replaced. Government regulations and systems to manage these transitions do exist and are well established. Let these regulations and processes work. There will be pain in this approach, but the pain will be greater if we continue to allow government intervention into private commerce. The reason our government cannot run a private-sector business efficiently or effectively is, in part, that it is not set up to do so. First, government organizations are political animals. Their primary interest is in satisfying a special interest, a key politician or oversight committee that controls their funding, or an important constituency. Customers, suppliers, and employees all come second to political interests; with no shareholders to please, being productive and profitable is just not a priority. In fact, government organizations take great pains to avoid measuring success. With no success metric, no one gets fired or reprimanded for poor performance. Next, government organizations are rule oriented, which means innovation and risk-taking are not in their nature. Finally, government organizations are established with a watchdog mentality. They are always looking over some other organization's shoulder, and someone is always looking over theirs. This mentality generates substantial unproductive expense and does not lend itself to building trust. Once the government owns a private-sector business, it will not compete fairly and will not let a bad (noncompetitive) business die if there is any political disadvantage in doing so. The government is not capable of efficiently or effectively operating a private-sector business (it can't even handle all the public business already on its plate), and it should not be allowed to own any part of any private business.

ॐ

Chapter 26

Man-made Global Warming

I do not pretend to know for certain if this concern is a real issue or just a political rationale for more government control of our lives, but I admit I am more than just a little suspicious. The issue of man-made global warming smells like a scare tactic designed to increase government control while it makes a few well-connected opportunists a great deal of money. Should it bother us that the last "hot" year was 1998, and that the temperature every year since has been the same or cooler? Should we ask why global-warming advocates changed the name from "global warming" to "climate change"? Don't we always have climate change? Does it make a difference that man-made global warming proof rests largely on computer models programmed by people who are man-made global-warming advocates? What should we think when the advocates say that if it gets warmer, it's global warming, while they also say that if it gets colder, it's still global warming? What will they say if the climate goes unchanged? Does it bother anyone that two of the most effective "fixes" (according to the advocates) for global warming are to stop eating meat and to have fewer kids? Does anyone notice or care that many of the man-made global-warming advocates create huge carbon footprints or that they have developed a scheme to buy and sell something they call "carbon offsets" that allows them to keep their planes, big cars, and huge homes while they attempt to eliminate yours? Is the science really settled just because global warming advocates say that it is settled? Where are the predicted hurricanes?

Be wary of the prophet making profit

It is also worrisome that global-warming support groups have become the last (or at least the latest) sanctuary for anti-Capitalists and antiestablishment refugees of all sorts, including Communists. It is also impossible not to notice and to accept as pure coincidence how the projected consequences of global warming fit so well into the Liberal political objective of increased government control. Plus, the proposed Liberal remedies for man-made global warming seem aimed at reducing commerce of nearly all kinds. I do not see my family living off the land—and off the grid. Throughout history there have been those yelling that the sky is falling. I am old enough to remember when global cooling and overpopulation were touted as destroyers of the world. H. L. Mencken said, "The urge to save humanity is almost always a false front for the urge to rule." Be wary of the prophet who profits from his message.

My suggestion is to have an extensive series of televised public debates between qualified scientists representing both sides of the argument. If man-made global warming turns out to be a legitimate issue, let's look for private-sector solutions. The bantering back and forth by politicians or CEOs who have a stake in the outcome is not helpful. It might be important to remember that both believers and nonbelievers in man-made global warming all favor reducing pollution. Continue to work on reducing pollution, but do not start spending money and creating new regulations until the country has heard the debates and the people have made an informed decision on this matter. If man-made global warming exists, the goal will be to fix it, not just to affix blame and achieve psychic satisfaction.

Chapter 27

Redistribution of Wealth

All true Conservatives recognize the need for a "safety net" for the truly needy, but it is the gradual creep of those not truly needy but those desiring to get a free ride that has to be discouraged. It seems completely unreasonable for the government (federal, state, and local) to be allowed to take as much as half of what an individual earns, but half is as far as I could go. No matter how much an individual makes, a dollar for the earner and a dollar to help others should be enough. If we allow the "free-riders" to continue to drink from the government well, we might soon find that, as **Senator Graham of Texas said, "We have too many wanting to ride in the wagon and not enough willing to pull it."**

Do not take so much from the achievers that the incentive to achieve is materially diminished or eliminated. These achievers are the people who create jobs and economic prosperity for the country. Let Capitalism work. Help the truly needy and those with severe disabilities who cannot help themselves, but set priorities. Make those who can provide for themselves do so.

251

Who will pull society? Who will work ten
or eleven months of the year for the government?

---

*The democracy will cease to exist when you take away from those
who are willing to work and give to those who would not.*

—Thomas Jefferson

Even in the most prosperous of economies and with the high
taxation it levies on half its citizens, our government doesn't have
unlimited resources. We cannot do everything that might be
helpful. We need to work with the people (not just the politicians)
to set clear priorities and force the politicians to stop spending when
they are out of money. The only exception to this is if immediate
supplemental money is needed to support a war where the country
is at risk of being severely damaged or overrun by our enemies. If
we must borrow, borrow responsibly.

It is too easy for politicians to buy votes with other people's
money. Our founders never intended to set up a system whereby

politicians could use OPM to buy power and perpetual reelection. Members of Congress were to serve at the ends of other successful careers as a form of giving something back to the country that had given them so much. The whole concept of "career politicians" might well be a significant part of our current problems. If the politicians want to spend beyond our means and the majority of voters want to let them, make it so the politicians who support this overspending have to contribute a material portion of their own income and net worth. If we are going to have redistribution of wealth as a policy, we need to begin by redistributing the wealth of our politicians. Redistribution of wealth is not a right contemplated by our founders or given to anyone by our Constitution. Redistribution of wealth is not a virtue unto itself. It is often just a populist way to buy votes to keep politicians in power.

෨෬

Chapter 28

Universal Health Care

This seems like a noble goal if we can actually manage it effectively and afford it. Put this program in with all the other noble programs such as Social Security, Medicare, Medicaid, unemployment insurance, endowment for the arts, defense spending, the IRS, the Department of Energy, the Department of Education, the National Parks (Department of the Interior), protecting open spaces and wildlife, the DMV, law enforcement, the State Department, NASA, judicial services, the Postal Service, and set priorities. *But don't buy it if we cannot manage and afford it.*

It is my sense that existing and expanded health-care programs will not survive without cost controls (including tort reform), choice, competition, and personal accountability. If we decide there is a need for universal health care or some other health-care reform, it seems like a terrible mistake to follow the failed example of Great Britain. The National Health Service of Great Britain now has approximately 1.4 million employees (most of whom are nonmedical staff, that is, not doctors or nurses) to serve a population of only 60 million. Only the Chinese Red Army and the Indian National Rail and its Ministry of Railways exceed a bureaucracy this size.

If you believe that health care is a public good to be guaranteed by the state, then a single-payer system is the next best alternative. Unfortunately, it is fiscally unsustainable without rationing.

—Charles Krauthammer, *Washington Post* columnist

It appears we might already have universal health care given the obligation of emergency rooms to provide medical treatment. It was reported in *Investor's Business Daily* that hospitals, including certain on-campus outpatient clinics and doctors' offices (those within 250 yards of the main buildings) are federally mandated to provide emergency treatment without bias toward legal status, nature of the infirmity, or capacity to pay. The Emergency Medical Treatment and Active Labor Act, a Health and Human Services department regulation, requires treatment be provided even when the medical problem is not an emergency. Further, these hospitals cannot discharge these patients until they are fully stabilized and have safe transportation. *We might be confusing* **universal health care** *with* **universal health insurance.**

We pay more for health care, in part, because we receive more medical treatment and we give more away to people who cannot or will not pay. **In an appearance on *This Week*, anchored by George Stephanopoulos, George Will queried, Are we looking for "2009 health care at 1959 prices? The problem with that is that 1959 health care was not very good."** The cost of "free" treatment is added to the invoices of paying patients or written off by the hospital. The cost of health care has also risen because of outrageous costs of malpractice lawsuits that from time to time produce lottery-sized judgments and huge attorneys' fees. Patients with real emergencies do need to be treated, and there must be consequences and compensation for malpractice; however, unfunded federal mandates for patient care and oversized financial rewards seem to bring with them their own set of problems. Hospitals are going out of business, especially in Liberal states such as California. Paying patients are footing the bill for services they did not even know existed. A spotlight needs to be shone on these costs so *we the people* can make an informed decision on how to address them. These are not matters that can be left solely to federal bureaucrats and our vote-buying political representatives. To battle this problem, make whatever insurance reform that applies to the people apply to all government employees and legislators.

There is often a lack of medical prudence shown when most of the health-care costs are paid for with someone else's money. As long as the doctor and the patient have no incentive for prudence, there will be very little of it. The underlying incentives related to health-care use and supply will likely need to change. The patient and the doctor cannot continue to be insulated from the true cost of health care or health insurance. Our current health-care payment system allows the doctors to focus primarily on the level of health insurance coverage and the patient to focus primarily on the co-payment. When neither the patient nor the doctor focuses on the total costs related to health care, including the cost of health insurance premiums often paid by employers, prudence will remain absent from the system.

The current and most of the proposed systems reward the use of more services whether or not the use of these additional services is prudent, and in the same way, these systems reward the use of more expensive medicines and tests. It also appears that none of these health-care plans rewards common sense healthful lifestyles or diligent prevention. Major tort reform is needed but will likely never occur given the lobbying power of personal-injury attorneys, especially if Liberals remain in power.

Health-care savings plans, along with catastrophic event insurance and nationwide shopping for health insurance, might be part of the solution. Medicare covers seniors and the disabled, Medicaid covers the poor, and government programs already exist for uninsured kids. The real question might be how to cover the uninsured people who aren't represented in these categories while still providing an incentive for them to get off government support as soon as possible. But it also might be helpful to remember that the government has no history of being able to reduce costs, increase quality, increase access, or run anything with efficiency. Do we really want government health care with the compassion of the IRS, the efficiency of the Postal Service, and the customer service of the DMV? Has anyone explained how we could add 30 million extra patients to the health-care system without adding more doctors, nurses, and hospitals? Can anyone explain why it is acceptable for the government to use an accounting system that uses ten years of revenues and compares it to six years of costs? Doesn't this wildly understate the costs? Plus, however quick the government is to provide additional service or assistance, the government is very slow to eliminate or even reduce these programs, even if they were put in on an emergency or temporary basis. If the government takes over health care, it will keep it.

ⅮⅯ

Chapter 29

Transparency
and Accountability

Quit talking about it and making empty promises. Eliminate such things as omnibus bills and any legislation that has unrelated tag-on amendments that allow any legislation to sneak through under the guise of something else. There's no reason for legislation about war funding to include preservation of endangered fish. Make each piece of legislation about just one thing and make every legislator and signer swear that he or she has read it. Eliminate any stealth programs that resemble anything like the middle-of-the-night earmarks designed to hide special favors put in place to pay off certain constituencies of senior legislators.

Reduce the tax code from 70,000 pages to twenty pages and make individual bills no longer than fifty pages. If there are more issues, offer up, debate, and approve more bills. In this way, it will be harder for politicians to hide legislative favors. Quit naming legislation in deceptive ways. Let no bill come up for presidential approval until it has been posted on the Web in its final form and with independent cost-benefit analysis for thirty days. Set up independent ethics hearings that do not involve legislators making judgments on their friends and fellow legislators. Stop allowing legislators to exempt themselves from certain laws and regulations. If we have to follow it, they have to follow it. Make all legislative compensation (including expense allotments or other funds under their control), perks, privileges, exemptions, and retirement benefits public in one easy-to-access place, and require prior approval from the people. Do not allow politicians to determine their own compensation and privileges.

How Stupid Do They Think We Are? Demand Accountability

Many believe that the above reformations can be accomplished only through the process of constitutional amendment. They believe that our present set of elected officials may complain about these issues but will never take any real action on them. Sadly, I agree.

೧෮ර

Chapter 30

Justices and Judges

Find a way to hold judges and justices accountable. The concept of lifetime appointments for federal judges and justices sounded like a good way to keep politics out of judicial interpretations and rulings, but it has not worked. Justices and judges do not always follow the law as it was written and originally intended. I am not quite sure how to fix this problem, but activist judges who make political or ideological decisions need to be held accountable. Judges who consistently prescribe very light sentences for serious felonies need to be removed. Perhaps lifetime appointments need to be replaced with seven- or ten-year appointments. Seven to ten years might be long enough to ensure some level of independence without giving a federal judge or justice carte blanche for life.

ာ

Chapter 31

Education

How difficult is it to measure educational success by measuring the level of student learning and achievement? Is this such a hard concept to comprehend or implement? The solution to improving education appears to lie in accountability for results. It begins with a focus on measuring how well children are learning the basics (reading, writing, and arithmetic), but it does not end there. Children also need to learn about science, philosophy, art, music, physical fitness, history, and civics, just to name a few subjects. Our current low performance in education is not merely the fault of the teachers or even the teachers' unions. The teachers are balancing their own interests with those of their students. Plus, they are working in a system that neither measures nor rewards success. The teachers' unions appear to be looking out solely for the teachers (not the kids), but looking out for the teachers is their job. They do not collect fees and dues from the kids or even their parents. Unions are businesses and union revenues are not affected by whether the teachers improve student learning or not; they collect their dues for improving teachers' compensation, benefits, and job security.

The important issue regarding teachers' unions is to take steps that will keep them from inhibiting any changes in the education system that will help improve teaching performance, as measured by how well the children learn the subjects. Is there a need for a union for kids? If we could find a way to fund this kids' union, perhaps this union could reward teachers not for getting more degrees or having more seniority, but for better teaching.

Parents are also a problem in many cases (some are not in the home, some are not educated, and some are not interested), but it seems this could be resolved by lengthening the school day (or adding a day) so there would be time and professional help to do that which otherwise would be relegated to homework. This extra time would allow the student to perform this study in a supervised and managed environment, and it would reduce the impact from unequal or disadvantageous home circumstances.

An important element strongly related to improving education is the objective, consistent, and relevant measuring of how well the children have learned each subject. Standardized tests might not turn out to be the best measure, but irrespective of whether these tests can be improved, standardized testing feels like a good start. Once a legitimate performance metric can be agreed upon, teachers who teach well (as indicated by how much their students learned during a specific time period) can be paid more. Many will fight measuring teacher performance by measuring student learning. And merit pay will also be fought because it also implies that those teachers who consistently underperform (assuming no extenuating circumstances) will receive less than others or might even be terminated.

In certain areas (e.g., Washington, D.C.), competition between the schools might be a good thing. In other areas where alternative schools do not exist, this might not be a factor. In any event, the whole notion of competition needs to be reintroduced into the school system for schools, students, teachers, administrators, and anyone else in the system. I understand that there are many who feel that competition might produce negative results for those who do not win, but this is the way of life. There are no design-neutral ribbons lauding adults for having shown up, and we don't receive "good job" accolades for every little thing we attempt. Sooner or later, all in the school will be out in the real world competing. One thing is for sure: the current system does not work well, and it needs to be improved.

෨෨

Chapter 32

Energy

Relying on energy sources that are not cost competitive or have yet to be refined or invented seems to unduly enhance the risk that our nation's energy independence might not meet a timetable that is consistent with our national security needs. The consequences of being held hostage by nations who hate us or who do not share our philosophy of liberty and freedom are both urgent and dire. No business would base its turnaround plans or its survival solely on unproven technologies, and no country should either. Does it bother anyone that almost all existing alternative energy sources produce less energy than they consume to create it? We have coal, we have natural gas, we have oil, and we have nuclear power. It appears we need to move forward at full speed on each of these fronts. It might be difficult for some to perceive or accept, but our country and its economy is based on inexpensive and bountiful energy sources. Today those sources include oil, natural gas, coal, and nuclear power.

This is not an argument for not pursuing new energy sources or new technologies to reduce pollution; in fact, the two strategies are not in any way mutually exclusive. As I understand it, alternative energy sources currently account for only 1 percent of our present-day needs. The extraordinarily narrow and exclusive focus on alternative energy sources seems like a bridge too far. If the argument is that oil, gas, and nuclear energy sources take too long to come to fruition, all that extra time the naysayers are projecting should be ample to reduce the side effects that many are so worried about. The idea that our government should work to raise the costs of our current sources of energy and punish all consumers (rather than increase the supply of energy) to justify the currently noncompetitive costs of alternative fuels seems un-American and foolish. In any event, noncompetitive costs are not the only problem with these alternatives.

There are many environmentalists who are against the use of fossil fuels or nuclear energy, who are also against miles and miles of photo-voltaic cells, against the miles and miles of gargantuan wind turbines, and against what they perceive as the untold disturbances to the environment of alternative energy transmission lines. Energy independence is necessary and serious. This is no time to rely solely on unproven methodologies and technologies. Pollution is one thing, but starving the entire Capitalist system and making our nation vulnerable to rogue nations is another. Work like crazy on technologies to reduce pollution, all the while building nuclear plants, drilling for oil and gas, and mining for coal like our livelihood, our independence, and our prosperity depend on it.

ை

Chapter 33

Foreign Policy

This is no time to abandon peace through strength, and it is no time to forget the sins of the past. Countries such as Iran and North Korea are seriously dangerous, and they are not the only ones. Russia is busy attempting to regain some of its lost Soviet Union respect and credibility. It is likely Russia will stick to its own neighborhood, but it might be risky to count on it, if for no other reason than the fact that it has a huge number of nuclear weapons. The Saudis are not on our side. They never have been. Syria is a terrorist nation. Peace is not close between Israel and Palestine. Venezuela is run by a tyrant who openly professes his hatred for America. Cuba still has a Castro. China is still run by Communists and owns much of our national debt. Pakistan is tribal and corrupt. Afghanistan and Iraq are still dangerous. Plus, there is al-Qaeda.

It is also no time to diminish our sovereignty by subrogating our nation's authority to international groups such as the often anti-American United Nations or to transfer it in the name of international treaties or the concept of transnationalism. There cannot be trust where no trust has been earned, and there certainly cannot be trust with organizations or nations that openly and vehe-mently oppose our values. International interests do not always line up with U.S. interests, and international treaties must be signed only when there is mutual advantage and our sovereign interests are protected.

∞

Chapter 34

Government Stimulus

I believe the private sector, not the government, will bring our economy back and keep it strong. Spending on infra-structure might be needed, but that spending will not create enduring jobs nor needed innovation in the marketplace. There has been much discussion on what some call trickle-down or trickle-up economics and endless debate on Keynesian versus supply-side economics. Arguments continue on whether govern-ment spending or tax cuts will be the more effective approach to dealing with this current recession and on which policy will better restore our economy to more normal levels of activity and prosperity. To me, the answer lies in the hands of the private sector. Given this belief, it seems to me that building bridges and giving money to community organizers will at best provide only short-term stimulus. The latest $800 billion "stimulus plan" looked more like political payoffs and radical left-wing programs than a job-creating bill. If most of the money won't be spent for years, why was the bill pushed through Congress in a matter of hours without due diligence of either public or legislative scrutiny?

It is doubtful much of it could have been passed without the deceptive guise and cover of a crisis solution. If we want to create jobs, we need to create incentives for entrepreneurs and others to create them. Raising taxes and increasing burdens on these potential job-creators just seems wrong. Capitalism is the vehicle for creating prosperity in America. It has been so for more than two hundred years.

An important key to economic growth and stability is innovation, which comes from the private sector (not government) and the supply-side of the equation. Consumers might have wanted better portable music or computing power, but they did not and could not have developed and distributed the iPod or the iPhone. Apple Corporation supplied the innovative products, and demand followed naturally. The government solution of attempting to borrow our way out of debt through deficit spending seems no more viable for the government than it would be for an individual household.

The government knows it is not an innovator, so it approaches our energy shortages like it approaches most problems. As stated above, it wants to increase regulations and reduce supply to raise the cost of current energy sources so the higher cost of alternative energy sources will seem more palatable to those who will have to pay them. In other words, the government is not looking to invent a new cost-effective energy source or invent a new pollution-reduction refining process; it wants to eliminate current low-cost options so it can replace them with the higher-cost alternatives that they prefer. This has been a common mistake of many Socialist nations.

The lifeblood of Capitalism is entrepreneurial risk-taking and innovation. If I could wave my magic wand, I would encourage entrepreneurial risk-taking and innovation by lowering taxes on business, allowing for immediate or at least accelerated depreciation of capital investments, and dramatically reducing capital-gains taxes. I understand that some of the tax reductions (e.g., capital gains) would likely pay for themselves by actually increasing tax revenues, and some of these tax reductions might actually reduce government revenues (at least in the short run), but this is a compromise I would make.

We need the enduring jobs that can come from only new products and services that can be generated only if we organize and encourage the millions of entrepreneurs in our country to join the fight. The government cannot innovate and government central planning will very likely make things worse. Government central planners have failed to correctly pick winners and losers for as long as they have been in existence. In fact, the government cannot help anyone without hurting someone else. The government does not create wealth; it only transfers it from one citizen who earned it to another who did not. When the government says it is putting money into this or that struggling or failing industry, it first has to take the money from some successful industry.

It is tough enough to effectively run a business when management is focused on the customer and the marketplace. It is next to impossible to effectively and successfully run a business when key decisions are based primarily on political concerns and public opinion. I also understand that a short-term reduction in government revenues might require us to borrow a bit more, print money a little more, and reevaluate our priorities, eliminating or reducing some government programs. But this is the road I would take.

Chapter 35

Housing Crisis

There is more than enough finger-pointing and placing blame for the current housing crisis. If finger-pointing is your purpose, take a number. Various media outlets (depending largely on their political bent) have reported that the housing downturn was caused by inadequate regulations, greedy Wall Streeters, politicians pushing low-income lending practices, corrupt or incompetent credit-rating agencies, the Federal Reserve Bank (which made cheap money too available), deceitful developers, and/or corrupt mortgage lenders. Plus, there have consistently been the somewhat more muted allegations about uninformed, misinformed, and even fraudulent consumers. Everyone on this list appears guilty.

One political side blames the crisis 100 percent on the Community Reinvestment Act, the attorney general's initiatives to prosecute or to threaten prosecution of bankers and other mortgage lenders who engaged in "redlining" (illegal discrimination in their loan approvals by not lending to people who could not or would not pay), and on key House and Senate leaders who pushed the government-sponsored entities (GSEs) of Fannie Mae and Freddy Mac to buy loans given to people who everyone knew could not afford them. These accusers also say that they tried to reform the GSEs but were blocked by the other side. The other side, of course, says that all of these allegations are either outright falsehoods or, if true, were not material to the crisis. They further respond by attempting to put all of the blame on the lack of adequate regulations, Wall Street greed, and big and corrupt mortgage lenders. It has become apparent that each side has a political point to make that attempts to gore the other's ox while protecting their own.

Clearly, there is much blame to go around. First of all, it appears to me that everyone (politicians, lenders, Wall Streeters, developers, the Federal Reserve, regulators, rating agencies, and citizens) who thought about the concept of making loans to people who could not afford to pay them back knew this was a bad idea bound for cataclysmic failure. I leave very little room in my own judgments for the notion that a significant percentage of people involved might have actually believed that the value of housing would keep rising forever and would, therefore, indicate any repossessed homes due to bad loans would be resold to others, probably for a profit. For those who say they tried to reform Fannie Mae and Freddie Mac, I say you did not try hard enough. You might have offered legislation or called for reform, but you did not stand on your desk and yell as if your hair were on fire.

As to inadequate regulations, there were some. Capital requirements were in many cases too low for banks or missing on certain securities offered by investment banking companies. Many derivatives (e.g., mortgage-backed securities and credit-default swaps) appear to have had practically no regulation or oversight. Most of these institutions (especially those with some form of government backing or guarantee) were too highly leveraged. But it looks as if many well-capitalized and well-regulated entities also failed because they just made bad loans, and many regulations actually required some lenders to make faulty loans.

So why was this allowed to go on? The answer appears to be that everyone was seeing substantial short-term benefits from these unwise lending practices, and they all wanted their share of the pie. The politicians wanted to tout increased home ownership (especially the increased home ownership by minorities), and they wanted to take credit for the increase in jobs, the reduced unemployment, and the increase in national economic output. Some politicians also wanted to use this unwise lending policy to buy votes. The lenders, the rating agencies, and the Wall Streeters were greedy and focused on only short-term financial gains. Many borrowers were likely uninformed or misinformed, but I suspect that many others just took advantage of the situation, knowing they were committing fraud or at least knowing they could not pay back the loans. The public at large who, at the time, was not completely unaware of these foolish lending practices, enjoyed the short-term prosperity from the entire economic stimulus created by housing sales. None of these groups were concerned about the consequences. Nearly everyone chose to turn a blind eye to the problem.

The fix for this housing crisis might be beyond my capacity to determine. However, I believe that although some new regulations might be needed, a market-based solution will likely be best. The solution lies in the fact that we double our population every fifty years or so, and this increase in population along with market-place pricing will eventually take care of the excessive inventory of existing houses. In time, the market will mend itself. The politicians were at the very least major players in the fiasco as they made unwise decisions, policies, and regulations either because of incompetency and arrogance or because they were trying to please a constituency personally important to them. It is hard for me to believe that these same politicians would now have the capacity to leave their political concerns behind, become educated in economics, and resolve our housing downturn. It seems to me that with all the current and pending repossessed homes for sale, the government will largely need to get out of the way and let the market take care of this excessive inventory problem.

ಐಂ

Chapter 36

Respect for Innocent Life

There might be no more controversial and polarizing issue in America than that of pro-life versus the pro-choice perspectives on the moral and legal status of abortions. The pro-life people generally believe that life begins at conception or perhaps, in some cases, at viability. In other words, they believe that once a child is conceived or a fetus is viable, a person with a soul lives and, therefore, demands societal protection. The pro-choice people appear to believe that life begins at birth or perhaps, in some cases, at viability. Therefore, they believe that societal protection is not warranted from the time of conception, and thus, societal protection is not demanded or required until birth or viability. Although there are many nuanced positions on this matter, the country appears to be somewhat evenly split on this issue.

Many pro-choice believers appear to feel that since the beginning of life, particularly life with a soul (for those who believe in the existence of souls), is scientifically undeterminable, the issue should rightfully be left to the mother. Many pro-life believers appear to feel that their religious teachings and often their consciences dictate that life begins at conception. Ronald Reagan said, ***"If government***

is to err, it must err on the side of protecting human life." I admit
that I am pro-life, and I agree with Reagan's words.

I do not know if it was my religious upbringing or my conscience
that has driven me to be pro-life, but I know that I am. I have the
sense that more people are moving to the pro-life position. I suspect
this shift in thinking might be due as much to new technology
(which more clearly shows the growth and maturity of a fetus) as to
shifts in religious beliefs. Clearly we know that viability exists long
before the natural full-length gestation time; from my perspective, it
appears that many people formerly of the pro-choice position have
now come to believe that the fetus deserves societal protection at
least at viability.

I understand that this is a political question having as much to
do with that which is considered by society to be morally permis-
sible and that which is considered by society to be morally wrong
as it has with any real legal issue. To me, it is unfortunate that a
few justices have interjected themselves into this debate because it
seems likely this issue will not be determined in churches, in the
legislature, or even in the judicial system. My sense is that it will be
settled, if it ever is, in the court of public opinion. In the meantime,
it is hard for me to believe that a majority of people can be against
parental notification or a ban on late-term abortions (especially
that procedure which is often termed as "partial-birth abortion").
In addition, it seems most could agree to facilitate and expedite
the adoption process and agree on educational programs designed
to prevent or to minimize unwanted pregnancies. Since nearly
everyone says that they would like to see a reduction in abortions,
perhaps these small steps are a way to start.

◈

Questions for Kids

1. Why do people argue about immigration?

2. Can and should government start a business?

3. Is there man-made global warming?

4. Where does the government get its money?

5. Why are the bills in Congress so long?

6. Are judges Republicans or Democrats?

7. How do we make our schools better?

8. Are insurance and oil companies bad?

9. Who or what caused the recession?

Part V

A Call to Action

Chapter 37

How Do You Know
Whom to Vote For?

Thjs was the question from my ten-year-old son that started me down the path of defining my own philosophy of life and politics. Although my actions and my political decisions have remained fairly consistent for many years, without Sammy's question, I might never have taken the time to do the extensive research necessary to refine my thoughts on these matters, and I might never have realized exactly why I feel as I do. It is my hope that as the lessons learned from history, experience, reason, conscience, and morality are rediscovered across America, that the philosophy of Common Sense Conservatism will appeal to everyday citizens across the country as much as it does to me. I know that nearly all parents look at many, if not all, of life's major decisions through the prism of how those decisions will affect their children, just as I do. I also suspect that most citizens have a positive opinion of our country and at least some level of belief in our people and optimism about the future.

I call my general and political philosophy *Common Sense Conservatism*. Common Sense Conservatism always begins by asking whether or not a potential or proposed government program or policy will work for our children—not how it is promised or intended to work, but *will* it work. It asks the same question of existing government programs and policies. The next question demanded by Common Sense Conservatism is about priorities (i.e., is this proposed or existing program more or less important to the safety, security, and opportunity for prosperity of our children than all other existing or proposed programs?). Common Sense Conservatism believes in the general goodness of our country and its people; however, this is not an argument to ignore the existence of wrongdoers in our midst. Part of the reason for my optimistic outlook for our future is my belief that ordinary citizens can and will eventually see through political deception. I believe in the preeminence of children, the vigorous expression of patriotism, and the power of clear-eyed optimism.

Vote for Someone who Believes in
Common Sense Conservative Principles

Common Sense Conservatism, with its focus on children, patriotism, and optimism, has given me renewed energy and added faith that I am ready to continue the tasks of engaging in how our country is being governed and in preparing my children for whatever future arrives. My recognition that it will not be long until our children are running the country was at first quite chilling. In spite of the fact that one is in and three are nearing high school, in many ways I still see my sons as toddlers. However, I see now that the future will depend both on what we leave them and on what they are able to contribute on their own. I also have a great deal of faith in the citizens (and especially the parents) of America. **We care, we are smart, and we will do this job right**.

It is up to you to decide the philosophy that is right and best for you and your kids. It is also up to you to make your own political decisions. You will have your own take on history, your own set of experiences, your own way of reasoning, and your own view of morality. We all need to engage in the process of how we are governed and to educate ourselves and our kids about the issues and the candidates. The candidates, irrespective of their rhetoric, will likely be in the future as they have been in the past. Discover their pasts and you can predict their futures. My hope is that we, and eventually our kids, will participate in the political process to avoid becoming victims of it. My expectation is that with Common Sense Conservatism as our guide, we will select candidates with character, enthusiasm, even temperament, and good values. We need to choose the person we feel is most capable and whose principles and lifestyle are consistent with our own set of values. It is my hope that many will read and consider what I call the *Common Sense Conservative Mission*.

The Common Sense Conservative Mission

*O*pen our eyes and look at America, as she exists today. Government policies are often devoid of proven principles, and the political process has become rigged and corrupt. Think about how our decisions will affect our children. Don't be afraid to engage in the process, to express your patriotism, or to communicate your optimism. Look at the shifting balance toward government power and away from the protection of individual liberties. Compare today's circumstances to the historical individual and collective opportunities for all Americans and recognize that much work remains to be done. However, in spite of high taxes, unnecessary regulations, deceptive politics, failing government institutions, and huge federal and state deficit spending, America's people are strong and America's future remains bright.

In pursuit of noble objectives, our country has temporarily headed down a path away from personal responsibility and toward the failed policies of too much government obligation and power. We the people have allowed our politicians to become openly deceitful, and this deception must be ended now. However, now is not the time to become discouraged or disheartened. No damage has been inflicted on our country or on our way of life that cannot be repaired with personal education, broad participation in the political system, and moral character.

The trail to American peace and prosperity was clearly marked by our founding fathers in the form of individual rights, maximum personal liberties, and limited governance. Now is the time for us to take control of our destiny and to become masters of our own fate. We need to peacefully but firmly remind our government representatives and officials that they work for us. We need to exercise our authority and obligation to return our political system to its original roots. Don't let anyone (including the government) take our lemonade stands. It is time, right here and right now, for all citizens (especially parents) to become educated and engaged in the political process, and to teach our children to become educated in the philosophies of life and politics and to think for themselves.

Peace and prosperity are not inconsistent with Common Sense Conservative principles, integrity, and transparency. We as American citizens must make it so.

America's Future Is Bright

Chapter 38

American Exceptionalism

I t seems odd to me that so many Liberals oppose the concept of American Exceptionalism. To Common Sense Conservatives, America occupies a special place among nations in part because of its unique history, economic and political opportunities, rejection of a ruling elite, individual liberties, equal treatment under the law, freedom of religion, support for Free-Market Capitalism, and constitutional republic form of government. The concept of American Exceptionalism does not mean that America has no flaws, that America has made no mistakes, that America should be judged by double standards, or that Americans are necessarily more capable than others. It reflects that America stands for a unique set of ideals and that America's belief in freedom, self-evident truths, and unalienable rights set it apart from other nations. As opposed to many other nations, when America has made mistakes, they were usually mistakes in means, not in objectives. In other words, America strives to do good, usually in the form of liberty and equality. America welcomes more immigrants than any other nation; more people who wish to emigrate from their native countries want to come to America than any other destination. This fact alone should tell us something about American Exceptionalism. In spite of all the evidence to the contrary, many Liberals see the concept of American Exceptionalism as self-serving propaganda that often results in a too-aggressive foreign policy. Liberals often have transnational perspectives and believe in world law, as opposed to national law. They see the notion of American Exceptionalism as a myth that includes excessive pride in country, and they see American ideals as no better than those of any other nation. Common Sense Conservatism is not afraid to express its patriotism or its optimism. Our country will do well because of our exceptional beliefs, and we will prevail precisely because of our unique history and ideals.

৫৫৫

Common Sense Conservatism:
The preeminence of children, the vigorous expression of patriotism, and the power of clear-eyed optimism

Chapter 39

Organize Your Thoughts, Develop Your Own Set of Principles, and Determine Your Own Course of Action

T
he original purpose of this book was to help me educate myself and my children regarding the choices we will have to make in politics and in life. It is now my expanded hope that other citizens and other parents will also find the ideas and notions expressed in this book helpful in developing their own philosophies and principles to guide their political and life choices. I want all Americans, including my and others' children, to be able to identify worthy objectives, focus on critical issues, analyze alternative means, and measure the success of programs and candidates they support. Admittedly, my perspectives and opinions are conservative, Common Sense Conservative. I have come to these views because I believe that Common Sense Conservative principles provide the best guide for all in society, including those in government. I do not argue, however, that all Conservative programs and initiatives have worked to my satisfaction. And I do not argue that all Progressive programs

and initiatives were flawed. My argument is that when Common Sense Conservative principles are applied to everyday, real-world problems, there is a much greater opportunity for success and that when objective performance measurements are applied to the many existing government programs, it will be clear that many need to be eliminated or significantly changed.

My sense is that too many people in America (especially moms such as me who are busy with kids, schools, work, and extracurricular activities) might not have done the research or spent the time to fully think through the issues facing us today. Given all of the problems facing families today, I completely understand this situation. I also feel that there might be too many uninformed or misinformed voters who have made their choices based on style and rhetoric rather than history and principles. Elections must stop being elaborate beauty contests. We must look at principles, policies, and character. I have talked to many friends and acquaintances who say they are not very political. By this comment, it appears they believe, as I once did, that political decisions might not be important to them. They seem to feel that "politics" just does not impact them or their families. Again, in the heat of day-to-day decisions, this, too, is understand-able. My hope is that the opinions and facts presented in this book will provide enough relevant input that some of these apolitical or even antipolitical perspectives might be changed. However, my real hope is that other citizens, especially other children (as well as mine), will get the sense that politics and civics, however distasteful and deceitful they might seem, are important.

ᕙᕗ

Chapter 40

Deception Is Rampant—
Set Your Goals High

I understand that I might have set my goals too high. Most politicians are cleverer than I, and they have become experts at spouting well-polled talking points. Their words might be misleading, but their arguments often seem quite compelling. They use words such as *trust, compassion, caring, hope, change, social justice,* and *fairness* to sell their messages. These words are powerful, but their use often (and perhaps, in many cases, intentionally) allows the casual listener to define the meanings and probable government programs behind them regardless of what the politician intends.

All men having power ought to be distrusted to a certain degree.

—James Madison

Progressives seldom call themselves Liberal, and they often use Conservative-sounding language to sell their platforms. Conservative politicians also use similar tactics, especially when they are talking to audiences with a Liberal bent. Republicans are not always Conservative, Democrats are not always Liberal, and Independents are almost never independent. No one in politics ever takes responsibility for their mistakes and failures unless they are caught on tape. They parse words and use shrewd semantics to blur their real intentions. They make promises they know cannot be delivered upon, and they make outrageous and exaggerated accusations about their opponents that they know to be untrue. In short, the political process is completely broken. I heard someone say the other day that for the past hundred years, many of the founding principles articulated by our founding fathers have been quietly ignored, purposely misinterpreted, or ruthlessly thrown aside. This could not be more true. I fully realize the difficulty in overcoming these adversarial tactics; however, I believe in the capacity of everyday citizens to overcome nearly any adversity, and I still believe it is worth the effort.

Never Pay a Politician (or Anyone Else) to Lie to You

Take Back Our Country Right Here and Right Now

Freedom has cost too much blood and agony to be relinquished at
the cheap price of rhetoric. —*Thomas Sowell*

Chapter 41

Education, Engagement, and Reason

I f you have read the book, you know that I believe that education, morality, engagement, and reason are the antidotes to our political and economic problems. Many have told me that because of the huge number of people working for the government or receiving government assistance that I am too late with this message. They believe that those depending on the government will never decide to support rugged individualism or self-reliance. Perhaps they are right, but I believe that although it is natural for people to want to take care of themselves and their families first, the average person still perceives a clear line between right and wrong, and in the long run, he or she wants to do that which is right.

As citizens and as parents, we need to look at everything with a critical eye and decide for ourselves so we can make the best decisions for our children, our country, and ourselves. My hope is that we will continue to educate ourselves about the historical successes and failures of both Liberal collectivism and Conservative individualism. We need to understand the foundations and the objectives of each, but the many politicians who call themselves Conservatives or Progressives but act as though they were the opposite cannot be allowed to fool us. We need to analyze the features and flaws of both philosophies and know why we believe one works and one does not. We need to take into account the lessons of history, and we need to think for ourselves and stay true to the philosophy we will have come to believe.

And if any of us chooses to run for political office, we need to take positions consistent with our principles and remain focused on helping all in society (and especially our children) maintain their unalienable rights of life, liberty, and the pursuit of happiness. If we choose to participate in politics primarily as a voter, we need to become fully informed voters and make sure that if a candidate is elected, he or she can set aside the desire for power, wealth, and prestige. Woodrow Wilson said, **"Every man who takes office in Washington either grows or swells, and when I give a man an office, I watch him carefully to see whether he is swelling or growing."** Pick one who will grow.

Prepare Yourself, Your Kids, and Our Country

Chapter 42

A Final Obligation

Our nation was founded on the concept of voluntary cooperative action. Government dictates stand in direct conflict with this notion. Conservatives support limited government, but "limited government" does not mean or imply no government. There is an important and valid role for government in society, and Conservatives support this role. However, Conservatives believe that too much government is as dangerous as too little. In addition, Common Sense Conservatives demand that government initiatives work.

I hope all citizens will consider this book a call to action!

What Can We Do?

1. Educate ourselves and our children about what has worked and what has not worked.

2. Recognize the limited resources of any organization (even one that is as large as our government).

3. Promote and demand fiscal responsibility (follow the five rules).

Sounds Good versus What Works

Much of the social history of the Western world, over the past three decades, has been a history of replacing what worked with what sounded good. —*Thomas Sowell*

4. Demand our government set priorities. We cannot do everything, so we must eliminate or modify programs that do not work. We need to do that which is most important to us, knowing that because of limited resources we will need to leave some good things behind.

5. Demand that the performance of government programs be fairly measured, with those measurements effectively communicated to the public in an accurate and timely manner.

6. Mobilize to support candidates who agree with our philosophy and abide by our principles; mobilize to defeat candidates who do not. Volunteer our time and money (if we can) to groups or candidates who support our issues.

7. Support the seventeen issues listed below.

8. Set up a list of friends to e-mail regularly on current issues.

9. E-mail and call our representatives in both the House and Senate. Let them hear our thoughts regularly.

10. Contribute to groups or organizations that think and act like we do.

11. Help register like-minded people to vote.

12. Teach our children the principles we believe in to prepare them to run our country.

13. Stay informed. Consult information sources that are balanced, not biased.

14. Cast an informed vote.

Seventeen Issues to Support

The following might well require a constitutional amendment:

1. Support six- or twelve-year term limits to eliminate career legislators.

2. Make Congress abide by any law it passes and imposes on the American people. Eliminate Congress's authorization to give itself pay raises or any form of increased compensation (require a vote of the people). Eliminate all forms of "gifts" to legislators and other government officials (including but not limited to junkets, speaking honorariums, and meals). Make Congress and all federal employees participate in Social Security like all other citizens (i.e., eliminate government pensions).

We the People Can Do It!

Get in the Game: Think for Yourself and Take Back
our Country Right Here and Right Now

3. Make English the official language of the United States of America, allowing exceptions for public safety and health reasons.

   Note: There is a huge cost (billions of dollars annually) to bilingualism, but this is not the primary issue. America is an immigrant country, and English as the official language would further assimilation into American society and the opportunity to advance. This is not an argument to ban any other language from America; it only recognizes that English is a key to full participation in the opportunities of America.

4. Reduce the power of the federal government by redefining "general welfare" as for the good of the majority of citizens, not just good for some citizens.

5. Redefine the legislative and judicial use of the "Commerce Clause" to reduce the level of federal government intrusion in state or citizen affairs.

6. Reduce our Tax Code to twenty pages, and require all legislative bills to address only one subject (no extraneous add-ons) using fifty pages or fewer. Eliminate omnibus bills and such items as earmarks.

7. Establish an independent ethics panel to review actions by legislative and other government officials.

8. Require schools to measure and reward success (success being defined by student learning and achievement). Deregulate the school system, and support charter schools and other scholastic innovations.

9. Prohibit the government from owning any private-sector business. Take government out of the bailout business.

10. Make illegal immigration *illegal*. Close our borders to terrorists, drugs, and criminals. Establish an immigrant work-permit program that requires background checks but treats existing immigrants with dignity and respect. Deport all immigrant felons. Rework immigration policy to include and support useful and valuable import of immigrants with needed skills.

11. Support energy independence. Use existing resources (e.g., oil, natural gas, nuclear power, and coal) while we continue to invest in research to reduce pollution and develop cost-effective alternative energy sources.

12. Develop metrics accepted by a majority of citizens for measuring the efficacy and performance of all

government programs. Place a sunset on all government agencies, entitlements, and programs. Make the public aware of their past performance metrics, and require reauthorization in full public view.

13. Require a supermajority to increase federal taxes or fees, and limit federal spending to 20 percent of GDP except for tightly defined emergencies.

14. Allow for a presidential line-item veto.

15. Post all legislation for twenty business days before voting is allowed.

16. Post all campaign contributions for five business days before allowing same to accrue to the candidate. Link all contributions to the contributor.

17. Ban all legislators from lobbying for ten years.

As a final note, I believe that those who believe in Liberal or Progressive political philosophy might well be mistaken, but I do not equate that belief to them being bad or evil people. Honorable people can have honest differences on complex subjects. We all know that it is possible and preferable to disagree with someone without personal attacks, without attacking motives, and without being disagreeable. The Common Sense Conservative argument against the Progressive agenda is that, however noble the objectives, more often than not, the means just do not work or the necessary resources are just not available. Common Sense Conservatives believe that the people really are more capable than the government and to unleash this capability, the government, with very few exceptions, needs to get out of the way. If you believe in the concepts of *children first, patriotism,* and *optimism,* Common Sense Conservatism might be your guide. Right now is the time and right here is the place for all of us to revisit the lessons of history and experience. Right now is the time and right here is the place to rely on our own capacity to reason and our own sense of morality. Americans of all persuasions are becoming more educated about our history and more disillusioned with our political class. With the help and engagement of we the people across the country, we can fulfill our civic and parental obligations and all join in the process of taking back our country to ensure that America's future is bright.

It is time to rethink our national agenda by using proven principles to address wayward policies and to eliminate corrupt political processes and practices. There is no good reason to allow American citizens to be squeezed by the government and no logic in continuing to allow the political system to be rigged against us when we the people have the power to change it.

Note to my boys, and to all boys and girls:

To my sons, and to other children, I say continue to be good citizens and act as gentlemen (or ladies) toward all. Do your part to improve not only our government, but also our society while you seek your own prosperity. Aspire to be good. Remember that the concept of doing well is not mutually exclusive with the concept of doing good. Engage in life regardless of the potential for criticism or failure. Remember the words of our twenty-sixth president, Theodore Roosevelt:

It is not the critic who counts; not the man who points out how the strong man stumbles, or where the doer of deeds could have done them better. The credit belongs to the man who is actually in the arena, whose face is marred by dust and sweat and blood; who strives valiantly; who errs, who comes short again and again, because there is no effort without error and shortcoming; but who does actually strive to do the deeds; who knows great enthusiasms, the great devotions; who spends himself in a worthy cause; who at the best knows in the end the triumph of high achievement, and who at the worst, if he fails, at least he fails while daring greatly, so that his place shall never be with those cold and timid souls who neither know victory nor defeat.

—Theodore Roosevelt, "Man in the Arena," April 23, 1910

Questions for Kids

1. What can everyday people do about how our country is run?

2. What can I do?

3. Are Americans special?

4. Why do politicians mislead us?

5. What issues are important?

6. What can my parents do about the government?

Don't Take My Lemonade Stand
An American Philosophy

Take Back Our Country
One Lemonade Stand at a Time

There's no question that our political system has become corrupt and politicians on both sides of the aisle are voting in favor of the special interests that donated to them instead of the citizens who elected them. They have all contributed to the abandonment of the Common Sense Conservative principles upon which our country was founded and under which we have prospered.

Here's the book that tells where we came from; how out-of-control, big-government/big-spending policies are driving us to ruin; and exactly what we the people can do to take back our country right here, right now. We can get it back on course toward peace, prosperity, and opportunity.

Right Here and Right Now

Appendix

Suggested Readings:

1. *A Conflict of Visions: Ideological Origins of Political Struggles* by Thomas Sowell

2. *The Vision of the Anointed: Self-Congratulation as a Basis for Social Policy* by Thomas Sowell

3. *Capitalism and Freedom* by Milton Friedman

4. *Free to Choose* by Milton Friedman

5. *Keeping the Tablets: Modern American Conservative Thought* by William Buckley and Charles Kesler

6. *New Deal or Raw Deal? How FDR's Economic Legacy Has Damaged America* by Burton Folsom, Jr.

7. *The Wealth of Nations* by Adam Smith

8. *Common Sense* by Thomas Paine

9. *The U.S. Constitution*

10. *The Declaration of Independence*

11. *John Adams* by David McCullough

12. *The Last Lion, volumes I and II,* by William Manchester

13. *Saving the Revolution* edited by Charles Kesler

14. *Patriotic Primer: A Patriotic History of the United States* by Larry Schweikart